SODOM

A Play in Two Acts

Isaac Bashevis Singer

Translated and edited by
Debra Caplan and David Stromberg

Cast of Characters (doubling and tripling permitted)

Abraham
Backstabber
Bastard
Bitchy
Boor
Citizen 1
Citizen 3
Citizen 3
Corrupt
Eldest
Friend
Guzzler
Slave
Looter
Lot
Lot's Wife
Maid
Oaf
Old Woman
Savage
Snitchy
Woman
Youngest
Young Woman

Editorial Preface

This play, found in Singer's archive, appears to be an original work, composed in Yiddish for the theater or radio. Unlike Singer's known productions, this work is based not on his stories, but on the biblical tale of Lot and the destruction of Sodom. Though it bears no date, it treats themes to which Singer returned over throughout his career.

Singer published a series of literary experiments as "Lot's Diary" in the *Forverts* in 1964, and a children's book, *The Wicked City* in 1972. But the play's style, as well as the quality of the paper, suggest it may have been written earlier, around the mid- to late-1950s, when he was preparing radio plays for the *Forverts* station, WEVD. It reveals the hand of a master storyteller deploying the power of dialogue with limited sets and directions. It exhibits Singer's ability to move between comedy, political satire, and spiritual sentiment, all within a play that is loyal to its biblical sources.

Singer reviewed theatrical productions under various pseudonyms, and often portrayed the Yiddish theater in fiction and memoir. Yet the extent of his own theatrical efforts is only beginning to be known. The length of the play, its construction, and its complex treatment of the days before Sodom and Gomorrah were destroyed, all betray the seriousness of Singer's preoccupation with the theater.

The play's themes, corruption and repentance, are portrayed with such canonical characters as Lot and Abraham, while shifts from comedic dialogue, to critiques of totalitarianism, to expressions of awe and faith, capturing the fear and trembling of the those who believe that they have seen the great powers of the Abrahamic God. In this sense, the play is both a biblical comedy and a spiritual affirmation of the human need for the Divine.

David Stromberg, Jerusalem

ACT I

Scene 1

A courtroom in Sodom. BASTARD the judge, LOT the defense
attorney, and GUZZLER the prosecutor. SLAVE brings in
three goblets of wine.

LOT: Wine!

BASTARD: Looking good today, Slave!

SLAVE: Must be the new makeup. You smear it on and
                your face turns shiny – like the beak of a crow
                that's just eaten devil's dung.

BASTARD: She's good at repeating the salesman's pitch.

LOT: With his smooth talking, he could convince you
                that shit smells like clover, piss is perfume, and
                corpses smell better than roses. In Sodom, if the
                salesman says it, it must be true.

GUZZLER: Lot, you're just like the rest of us. You're more of
                a Sodomite than any anyone else in Sodom. You're
                just casting stones into your own well.

BASTARD: Once a foreigner, always a foreigner. He shouldn't
                forget that Abraham, that Hebrew, is his uncle. If
                you're like Abraham and his god so much, why
                live here in Sodom? Go get circumcised and live
                with him in Mamre. You can't have one foot here
                and another foot there.

LOT: You take things too seriously, my friends. I love
                Sodom. My life would have no meaning if I had to
                leave. Sodom is the only place where I can
                breathe. My family finds fault in everything. But
                I say: let Sodom be Sodom.

GUZZLER: Being critical used to be a good thing. But now,
                when the people of Gomorrah are preparing to
                attack us, and even our allies in Adma and
                Zeboim are spreading lies about us, we need to
                stick together. But Lot, you're always on
                Gomorrah's side. You see their virtues and our
                vices. Why don't you go live in Gomorrah if you
                like them so much?

LOT: Me? Live in Gomorrah? You must be joking. In
                Sodom, people can still say whatever they want.
                In Gomorrah, if you say one wrong word against
                the Leader or his court, they smear you with
                honey and send you to the bees. Flattery doesn't
                help, either. My cousin was a singer in the
                Leader's court, the greatest flatterer in Gomorrah,
                but they hung him – without a trial.

GUZZLER: Why?

BASTARD: He probably poisoned the honey. Abraham's
                people can never be trusted. They find fault with
                everything. Which is why I say they should go to
                Canaan and stay there.

LOT: These kinds of statements undermine the very
                foundation of this kingdom.

SLAVE: Why aren't the gentlemen drinking? The wine is waiting. . .

LOT: Let's drink. To your health – and to Sodom's prosperity! May it grow and may there be peace between Sodom and Gomorrah.

GUZZLER: We can only have peace with Gomorrah if we give them everything: our gold, our silver, our houses, our very lives. You know this, Lot, but you keep talking about peace. Of all the liars in Sodom, you lie the most.

LOT: Since when is lying a problem in Sodom? (Everyone laughs.)

BLACKOUT. Two sisters are led in, an adult and a fourteen-year-old.

BOOR: We have a lot of murder trials today, so I'll make it short. For a year, these two sisters – Snitchy, who's thirty (or so she says), and Bitchy, who's fourteen – lived with their lover, Looter. A month ago, Looter was found decapitated. The charges are that Snitchy committed the murder because she was tired of Looter and he wouldn't leave, but when the police came, her little sister Bitchy took the blame. They say that while Snitchy was sleeping, the younger one hacked off Looter's head with an axe. Their intention is obvious: Bitchy's a minor and can't be punished, since according to the laws of Sodom, minors can kill whoever they want, as much their hearts desire.

BASTARD: What do you have to say, Guzzler?

GUZZLER: It's not easy for a fourteen-year-old child to hack
                off someone's head with this much skill. A girl of
                fourteen doesn't have the strength. If she were to
                hack someone's head off, it would come out
                uneven. But Looter's head was chopped off by an
                expert. Everyone of Sodom was impressed by how
                well it was done. Such skill, such talent, such
                strength. All the experts praised her. Snitchy
                received bouquets of flowers and expensive gifts.
                Poets composed verses praising her. It's clear to
                everyone that Snitchy hacked off Looter's head,
                not Bitchy.

BASTARD: Lot, what do you have to say?

LOT: I will demonstrate that the prosecutor's words
                have no substance. His claim – that a young girl
                of fourteen does not have the strength to chop off
                a head as it ought to be done – is false. We have
                twelve-year-olds and even ten- and nine-year-olds
                who commit astonishingly good murders. Let's
                not fool ourselves – we teach our children how to
                chop off heads at an early age. As soon as they
                learn to speak, we start reading them scrolls that
                describe all kinds of murders. We teach them how
                to murder in school. We show them plays about
                how the greatest leaders stab, cut, hang, torture,
                and shoot people with bow and arrow. The
                prosecutor's words spit in the faces of our children
                and their teachers. If the court would like, I could
                provide a long list of children who have
                committed famous murders.

BASTARD: Not necessary. The court knows all about them.

LOT: Now, with the permission of the court, I will
                present witnesses.

BASTARD: Go ahead.

LOT: Snitchy, tell the court the truth (winks).

SNITCHY: The truth is: I was sleeping innocently when my
                little sister did it. I woke up in the morning and
                saw that Looter lay next to me without his head.

BASTARD: Did his screaming wake you?

SNITCHY: He didn't have time to scream.

BASTARD: Did you call the police?

SNITCHY: Not right away.

BASTARD: Why not?

SNITCHY: I was hungry.

BASTARD: Why have the poets written you love songs and
                not your sister?

SNITCHY: Who takes poets seriously around here?

LOT: If the court will allow it, I will present another
                witness: the beautiful and innocent Bitchy.

BASTARD: Yes.

LOT: Bitchy, tell us what happened that night. How
                did you kill Looter, and why did you do it?

BITCHY: My sister was spending too much time with him.

GUZZLER: You loved him too?

BITCHY: Sure. You don't kill someone you don't love. Even
                a baby knows that.

GUZZLER: Show us how you chopped off his head.

BITCHY: Give me an ax and I'll show you.

BOOR: Here.

BITCHY: *(Picks up the ax. The men tremble.)* Like this.

CROWD: How graceful! Look how she holds the ax. She'll
                soon surpass her sister! *(Someone throws her a
                bouquet of flowers).*

BASTARD: Prosecutor – do you have witnesses?

GUZZLER: I have no witnesses. When we want to chop off
                someone's head around here, we do it without
                witnesses. But, I have the head. I will show the
                court that a girl of fourteen could not do this, no
                matter how studious or well trained.

BASTARD: The head? Isn't it rotten?

GUZZLER: It's been preserved.

BASTARD: Well, show us.

GUZZLER: Here it is!

BASTARD: Lovely cut!

GUZZLER: An expert cut!

CROWD: So lovely! Looter himself couldn't have done it
                better! Is it for sale? I want it for my house! Why
                should you have it? Why can't I have it?

BASTARD: Quiet! This is neither a marketplace nor a shrine.

GUZZLER: This head is testimony to the hand that hacked it
                off.

LOT: Put the head away, Guzzler, and Bitchy will show
                you how strong and steady her hand is.

BASTARD: This is a court, not a tavern. This is no place for
                jokes.

LOT: The court should feel her hand and see how strong
                she is.

BASTARD: Show me your hand, Bitchy.

BITCHY: Here.

BASTARD: Ow, it hurts!

LOT: You don't understand the new generation. We
                raised them on milk and honey. The things we
                learned at thirty, they knew at seven. I ask the
                court to free her.

SNITCHY: They've been torturing the child for weeks and
                they won't leave her alone. What do they want?
                She killed Looter and he's dead. Nobody can bring
                him back to life. So what's the point of all this? I
                don't have time and she doesn't have time either.
                She should go back to school.

LOT: What will happen to our children if we keep
                dragging them through the courts? In Gomorrah,
                they don't have a lot of food, or shoes, or clothes,
                but they teach their children – and that's where
                their power lies. But we hold our children back.

BASTARD: Don't compare us with Gomorrah. This is a court,
                not a place for debate.

LOT: I think the world of Sodom.

BASTARD whispers something in BOOR's ear.

BOOR: Everyone out, except for Snitchy. *(Everyone
                leaves).*

BASTARD: Snitchy, it's common knowledge that you're the
                murderer, not your sister. It's a secret that

everyone in Sodom knows. Looter had rich
relatives and they've asked us to hang you.

SNITCHY: How much did they give you? I'm not as rich as
             you think.

BASTARD: You have the richest lover in Sodom.

SNITCHY: No matter how much you earn, it's never enough.
             Everyone rips you off. More than half of my
             paycheck goes to taxes. My slaves steal from me,
             my servants steal from me. Someone has to pay
             the man walking around singing my praises. And
             how much does makeup and perfume cost? Our
             money isn't what it used to be. The minters mix
             silver with lead and gold with copper. A coin
             from Sodom is barely a coin.

BASTARD: You think I don't know that? But I have my own
             expenses. The government doesn't pay judges
             enough. One of my lovers costs more in a week
             than I make in a month.

SNITCHY: This murder has cost me a trunkful of cash. Lot
             alone costs a fortune.

BASTARD: This murder made you important. Your name's on
             everyone's lips.

SNITCHY: Speak clearly, Judge. What do you want?

BASTARD: You're wearing an expensive brooch.

SNITCHY: I inherited this brooch from my mother. It's also
                my good luck charm. It gives me strength and
                hope. Without it, my life would be meaningless.

BASTARD: Give me the brooch.

SNITCHY: Never!

BASTARD: If so, you'll be hung. Tomorrow the vultures will
                eat the flesh from your skull.

SNITCHY: I'm not afraid of you. You can't hang me. I have
                all of Sodom at my feet. You know this.

BASTARD: When they hang you, you'll no longer have them
                at your feet.

SNITCHY: They'll take revenge.

BASTARD: Sodom has a short memory.

SNITCHY: How can I give it to you? What will the people
                say when I leave here without a brooch? After all,
                you're supposed to be a respectable judge...

BASTARD: When will I get it?

SNITCHY: Let me go – and I'll send it with a servant.

BASTARD: Sorry, Snitchy, but I don't believe a word you say.

SNITCHY: And what if I give you the brooch and you still
                sentence me to death?

BASTARD: It's come to this. Nobody believes anyone anymore. In my time, people still believed the word of a judge.

SNITCHY: In my time, there were still a few respectable judges.

LOT: *(Appearing at the door)* What are you two arguing about?

BASTARD: Who let you in?

LOT: I can leave.

BASTARD: Since you're here, come closer. This Snitchy of yours doesn't believe. . .

LOT: I heard everything, that's why I came in. She doesn't believe you, you don't believe her, but everyone believes Lot. You give me the brooch, Snitchy, and when he frees you, he'll get it. Does that sound fair?

BASTARD: Do you promise?

LOT: I swear by the gods.

BASTARD: So you do believe in the gods? Didn't your uncle Abraham destroy his father's idols?

LOT: Shouldn't I swear on something?

BASTARD: People like you can't swear on anything. (Calls out) Boor, call everyone in.

BOOR: Enter.

BASTARD: It's clear as day that Bitchy, not Snitchy, chopped
                 off Looter's head. Snitchy will be set free.

VOICES: Justice! Mazel tov! Where's her brooch? She
                 bribed him!

BITCHY: Snitchy! (Hugs her)

VOICES: Bitchy! Bitchy!

BITCHY: What do you want?

LOT: (Someone gives him a medal) Bitchy, the Society
                 for Chopping Off Heads has just awarded you a
                 medal. There will be a feast in your honor.

BITCHY: Thank you. May the gods reward you.

SNITCHY: You should be thanking me, not them.

BITCHY: Sister! (They embrace and leave)

BASTARD
The day's not over yet. Boor, call in the others.

BOOR: (Bringing in two young men) This is Corrupt and
                 this is Backstabber. Corrupt is accused of spying
                 for Gomorrah. He's giving away our secrets. He's
                 inciting slaves to rebel against us. Backstabber is
                 accused of the same crime, but there is evidence

that he's broken with Gomorrah and is back on
our side.

BASTARD: According to our laws, citizens can be on
                whatever side they choose. Treason is not a
                criminal offense.

CORRUPT: Am I free to go?

BASTARD: Sure. *(Pause)* Is it true, Backstabber, that you
                became one of them and then left?

BACKSTABBER: Yes, Your Honor.

BASTARD: Why did you come back?

BACKSTABBER: I was in Gomorrah and saw what was happening
                there. It was bad enough in Sodom, but
                Gomorrah was even worse.

BASTARD: What was worse?

BACKSTABBER: Everyone's a slave to the government. No one's
                free. If you want to take a shower, you have to get
                the government's permission. The government
                dictates everything: what you eat, what you drink,
                when you sleep, and who you sleep with. You
                even have to get permission to scratch yourself.

CORRUPT: May I say something?

BASTARD: Go ahead.

CORRUPT: He's a liar, a traitor, a snake. There's only one free
                country, and that's Gomorrah!

BASTARD: What do you think, Guzzler?

GUZZLER: I have nothing against Corrupt. The truth is, he'd
                like to kill us all, but who doesn't want to kill
                everybody else around here? I'm glad we
                acquitted him. On the contrary, I think he
                deserves a reward.

BASTARD: Why?

GUZZLER: The people of Gomorrah should know that we're
                nothing like them. In Gomorrah, when people
                support us, they get smeared with honey and sent
                to the bees. But we're not afraid of traitors. We
                treat our enemies better than our friends. We
                reward bad with good.

BACKSTABBER: You also reward good with bad.

BASTARD: Be quiet or we'll cut out out your tongue.

CORRUPT: The sooner the better.

BASTARD: What do you say, Lot?

LOT: We can't go against the law.

BASTARD: What do you think we should do with
                Backstabber?

LOT: He's neither ours nor theirs. If Gomorrah defeats
                    us in a war, Corrupt would be one of our judges,
                    and maybe he'd remember that we took good care
                    of him and he'd take care of us too. But what can
                    we expect from someone like Backstabber? He's
                    not useful. The people in Gomorrah hate him, he
                    says he wants to repent, but Sodom doesn't
                    believe in repentance.

BASTARD: Still, you have to defend him, that's your job.

LOT: If I must, then I will. I believe that Backstabber
                    has committed two crimes. First he was against
                    Sodom, and now he's against Gomorrah. But our
                    court is compassionate and will not judge him for
                    his transgressions. Let's send him back to
                    Gomorrah and see how merciful they are. If they
                    smear him with honey and send him to the bees,
                    everyone will see that we're good and they're bad.

CORRUPT: A good verdict!

GUZZLER: No matter what we say about you, Lot, you're
                    definitely smart.

BACKSTABBER: Better to be hung here than sent back there.

BASTARD: Are you going to tell the court what to do? Take
                    him, Boor, and tell the guards to send him to
                    Gomorrah.

BOOR: Come on!

BACKSTABBER: Murderers, liars, dogs!

GUZZLER: He's still on their side.

CORRUPT: Soon he won't be on any side. *(Sticks out his tongue to the side as if being hung. BOOR, CORRUPT, BACKSTABBER leave).*

BASTARD: That's Sodom for you. Never satisfied. Guzzler, you can go. Let's take a break.

GUZZLER: I'll be dining with your wife again today.

LOT: I'll see you both at my place tonight.

BASTARD: Lot, stay for a minute.

GUZZLER: The brooch, huh? *(Leaves)*

LOT: You want to talk about the law, Judge?

BASTARD: Where's the brooch?

LOT: What brooch?

BASTARD: Snitchy's brooch.

LOT: I don't understand what you're talking about.

BASTARD: Have we really sunk so low? The world's coming to an end.

LOT: Don't worry, Judge. I have the brooch. We're in
                Sodom, not Gomorrah. A promise is still a
                promise. But where's my payment?

BASTARD: You got enough money out of Snitchy.

LOT: According to Sodomite custom, I'm still owed a
                third.

BASTARD: What can I do? Take one of the gems off the
                brooch and give it to you?

LOT: What about a piece of the woman who will get
                the brooch?

BASTARD: You're a great many things, but you're no fool.
                Like everyone in Abraham's family.

LOT: You can't forget my family even for a second.

BASTARD: I know you're ashamed of them. It's easy to hit
                you where it hurts.

BLACKOUT.

Scene 2

BITCHY's house. OAF dances a wild dance with BITCHY.

BITCHY: Not so fast, Oaf. You're pulling me apart. My
                brain's about to fall out of my skull.

OAF: It's the hottest dance in Sodom. It's deathly. These
                two girls, both students of mine, broke their
                Necks and backs doing this dance.

BITCHY: It's a great dance, and really dangerous, but I have
                to learn it first. What are the rules?

OAF: The rules are that there are no rules. Dance, jump,
                throw your head and feet around – then scream.

BITCHY: What should I scream?

OAF: Whatever comes out of your mouth. And if you
                can, pick me up, and turn me upside down.

BITCHY: You're too heavy.

OAF: A young woman who could chop off Looter's head
                should be able to pick up a man like me.

BITCHY: You're making fun of me. Everyone's laughing,
                and you are too.

OAF: In Sodom, you have to laugh all the time. We live
                on laughter.

BITCHY: When I see how much respect people give Snitchy
                and how many presents they bring her, it makes
                me want to cry.

OAF: Are you jealous?

BITCHY: Ever since she killed Looter, she only sees
                important people. Poets praise her. Sculptors

sculpt   her. Goldsmiths put her face on jewelry. But I'm just the little sister. Remember this, Oaf – Bitchy will soon show Sodom who she really is.

OAF: What will you do?

BITCHY: Can you keep a secret?

OAF: If I revealed everything I knew, Sodom would fall apart.

BITCHY: I'm actually going to chop off someone's head.

OAF: Whose?

BITCHY: Snitchy's.

OAF: Really?

BITCHY: How much longer will I be a minor? As long as I'm under eighteen, I can do anything without consequences. After that, I'll have to bribe the judges and everyone else.

OAF: When are you going to do it? *(Kisses her)*

BITCHY: Soon.

OAF: Want me to help you?

BITCHY: No. I can do anything Snitchy can. Since she has no husband or children, we'll get the whole inheritance.

OAF: We will?

BITCHY: If you marry me.

OAF: You told me you were sick of men.

BITCHY: I want a child. Without children Sodom can't be
                  Sodom. Our servants are multiplying, and we, the
                  rulers of Sodom, have no time for children. People
                  spend so much time talking about sex that they
                  never actually have sex.

OAF: You know all the right things to say.

BITCHY: I'm going to use the same ax that Snitchy used.

The door opens. It's SNITCHY.

SNITCHY: Have you finished dancing? I was worried that
                  you'd bring down the house with all of your
                  stomping.

OAF: You're covered in flowers.

SNITCHY: Sodom's gone wild celebrating how she (pointing
                  to BITCHY) took care of Looter. But what did he
                  ever do to them?

OAF: People like blood.

SNITCHY: Women like it when men bleed, and men also like
                  it when men bleed. In the end, Sodom is turning
                  into a kingdom of women. Every man in Sodom
                  has three wives. There are almost no old men in

Sodom. They kill each other and leave everything to us.

OAF: What will you do without men?

SNITCHY: We'll get along with each other. Someday Sodom's men will be in chains, like wild oxen, and we'll only use them for procreation. Sodom will be ruled by a woman. Women will be the judges. They'll take up swords and fight wars.

OAF: With whom?

BASTARD appears at the door. SLAVE follows with a pitcher of wine and a bouquet of flowers.

SNITCHY: It's the judge!

BASTARD: I've come to wish you well and give you a present. During the trial, your innocence rose to the surface like oil on water. May I come in?

SNITCHY: Thank you, judge, for your gift and well wishes, but I can't receive anyone today.

BASTARD: Why not?

SNITCHY: The door is opening and closing all day long. Sodom's noblemen come to congratulate and kiss the hem of my dress. The praise from the poets is deafening. There's no country where people love justice like Sodom.

BASTARD: Should I come back tomorrow?

SNITCHY: Wait a few days, judge, until things die down.

BASTARD: In the courtroom, I'm a judge. But when I leave
               the courthouse, I'm a Sodomite like any other. I
               love beauty, and cunning, and women's sly ways.
               As a judge I look for the truth and weigh right
               and wrong on the scales of justice. But when I
               take off my judge's robe and hat, I laugh at all
               that nonsense. I want to tell you, Snitchy, you're
               famous. All of the young women in Sodom are
               jealous of you and want to follow your example.

SNITCHY: Let them. You'll have more people to put on trial.

OAF: Judge, I know I'm young, but let me say
               something.

BASTARD: The younger you are, the more you know. There's
               nothing worse in Sodom than being old.

OAF: If we celebrate every woman who cuts off her
               lover's head, soon we'll all be headless. It could
               even happen to a judge.

BASTARD: Anything can happen. But let's enjoy ourselves in
               the meantime. Around here, blood is sweeter than
               wine. Blood smells better than any perfume.
               When I wake up in the morning, the first thing I
               ask my slaves is whether anyone's been killed
               overnight. Isn't that right, Slave?

SLAVE: Yes, sir. The judge wakes up to news about
                  murder, and goes to sleep to news about murder.
                  Sometimes, when my master can't sleep, one of
                  the slaves reads him a history book where Sodom's
                  grisliest murders are recorded, and it lulls him to
                  sleep.

GUZZLER appears at the door, carrying a bouquet of flowers.

BASTARD: You too?

SNITCHY: The prosecutor's also here to wish me well?

GUZZLER: In the courtroom, I'm a prosecutor, but –

SNITCHY: But when you take off your prosecutor's robe and
                  hat, you're a Sodomite like all Sodomites.

GUZZLER: How did you know what I was thinking?

SNITCHY: You all sing the same song. Why are you carrying
                  these gifts yourself? Don't you have slaves
                  anymore?

GUZZLER: My wife keeps all the slaves for herself.

SNITCHY: The great prosecutor, who makes everyone quake
                  in fear, can't stand up to his wife?

GUZZLER: Women rule Sodom. It's their city.

SNITCHY: Well, thank you for the flowers and gifts.

GUZZLER: May I come in?

BITCHY:	No, you can't. My sister's tired. You're not the first today, and you won't be the last.
SNITCHY:	Now she's speaking on my behalf.
BITCHY:	Soon I'll be speaking for myself.
GUZZLER:	Why are you so full of yourself? You're not the one who murdered Looter.
BASTARD:	The court ruled that she did.
OAF:	Someone else is coming.
SNITCHY:	Who?
OAF:	Lot.
BASTARD:	And I thought that all Abraham's relatives wanted was money.
GUZZLER:	They want everything and so they punish everyone and keep talking about all kinds of disasters and destruction.
LOT:	*(Enters)* Hello everyone! Who's here? What are you all doing?
BITCHY:	Where are your gifts?
LOT:	Gifts for whom? For her – or for you?
BITCHY:	Who am I? The little sister of the great Snitchy?

LOT::   Don't put yourself down, Bitchy, there are enough
             fools in Sodom who believe that the court's
             verdict was just.

BASTARD: He's always making light of everything, always
             using double-talk. He supports the court and
             opposes the court, he supports the gods and
             opposes the gods, he supports Sodom and
             supports Gomorrah. Why don't you pick a side?

GUZZLER: Why? The wind's always changing. Wherever it
             blows, that's where Lot goes.

LOT: I know that you hate my family. You can't help
             but be jealous of our knowledge and instincts.
             But I'm telling you that Sodom's end is coming. I
             sense the smell of burning. At night, when I shut
             my eyes, I hear cries and see fires and smoke
             rising like from a furnace.

GUZZLER: And who will bring this destruction? The gods?

LOT: Why involve the gods? The destruction will come
             from Gomorrah, and not because they're smarter
             than we are. We're a small city of nobles, each
             with our own whims and desires, and they are a
             united mass. For them, the Leader's word is holy.
             He's the god of all gods. They'll attack us in the
             middle of the night when we're lying with our
             wives, or with each other, and they'll hack us to
             pieces.

SNITCHY: The men and the old women, not the young
             women.

LOT: They'll take the young women for themselves.

SNITCHY: They say that the men of Gomorrah have more
                power in their loins than the men of Sodom.

BITCHY: By the time this happens, sister, you'll be too old.
                They'll slash you with their swords and take me as
                their loot.

SNITCHY: Thank you, little sister, for your kind words.
                (Pause) What do you want, Lot?

LOT: May I come in?

SNITCHY: I'm tired, but come in for a bit.

BASTARD: She didn't have any time for me.

GUZZLER: She didn't even let me say what I'd prepared.
                (Pause) Tell me, Lot, how come you're so
                successful with women? You're not good looking,
                you're not powerful, you can't fight, you don't
                hunt. What's your secret?

LOT: Noah had three sons – Shem, Ham, and Japheth.
                Each had a different virtue. Japheth was
                handsome, Ham was passionate, and my ancestor
                Shem had a name for everything. His power was
                in his tongue.

GUZZLER: What kind of power is that?

LOT: Sodom likes to gossip. Our hands are idle. The slaves do our work. When we want to go somewhere, we ride a donkey. Our tongue is the only organ that does anything, and where the tongue reigns, Lot is king.

BASTARD: A tongue can be cut out.

LOT: But its words can't be unheard.

OAF: What happens to the words?

LOT: They each have a Sodom of their own.

GUZZLER: If you dislike Sodom so much, why don't you go to your uncle Abraham?

LOT: My head belongs to Abraham, but my heart is with you. Come on, Snitchy, I need to talk to you.

SNITCHY: Let's talk. *(They leave)*

OAF: Let's dance, Bitchy.

BITCHY: Teach me.

GUZZLER: Come on, Bastard.

BASTARD: Let's walk together. It's too dangerous to walk alone. There are murderers, thieves, and robbers everywhere.

GUZZLER: Well, you freed them all.

BASTARD: The prisons are full. We can't put everyone in jail.
                 (They leave. OAF and BITCHY dance)

                          Scene 3

*At Lot's house, in the garden. Lot's older daughter, ELDEST, and
CORRUPT.*

ELDEST: My father would be horrified to see us together.
                 He'd yell and lecture me. But he ought to know
                 the truth. You'll laugh, Corrupt, but he thinks
                 I'm a virgin.

CORRUPT: That's one of the craziest things about this town.
                 Everyone's corrupt to the core, but they want
                 their daughters to be innocent. This hypocrisy
                 will destroy Sodom.

ELDEST: How is it in Gomorrah?

CORRUPT: In Gomorrah, we don't do this kind of thing
                 anymore. We've destroyed all the gods and
                 worship the land. The Leader tells us that
                 everything is part of the land: the people, their
                 thoughts, their desires, their dreams.

ELDEST: What about the sky? Is that part of the land too?

CORRUPT: There's no sky. The sky is just the reflection of the
                 ocean.

ELDEST: And the sun? The moon? The stars?

CORRUPT: They're all fires that come from the land.

ELDEST: And where did the land come from?

CORRUPT: The land is the beginning of everything -- dark,
               blind, harsh, senseless, without a will, without a
               purpose.

ELDEST: And where do people and animals come from?

CORRUPT: It rained and got muddy – and when the mud
               warmed up, there were worms, mice, donkeys,
               and people carved out of it.

ELDEST: If the earth is blind, cruel, and senseless – why
               should we worship it? Can it hear our prayers?
               Can it smell our sacrifices?

CORRUPT: It's like we worship the earth, but really we're
               worshipping the myth. The Leader is the son of
               the earth. His orders are holy. Whoever he tells us
               to kill, we kill. Whoever he tells us to hurt, we
               hurt. When god is no longer god, man becomes
               god, and who's greater than our Leader?

ELDEST: And what about when the Leader is wicked and
               uses his power to do evil?

CORRUPT: There's no such thing as good and evil – no truth
               or lies. There's only power. People in Sodom know
               this, but hide it behind smoke and mirrors. Our
               faith in power is pure, and that's why Gomorrah
               will triumph.

ELDEST: Do you think there will be war?

CORRUPT: War is inevitable. But as long as we're not ready,
                we'll keep talking about wanting peace.

ELDEST: Then you're all liars.

CORRUPT: Our Leader has taught us that whatever serves our
                goals is the truth.

ELDEST: Tell me, when you get power, will you at least
                spare my father's life?

CORRUPT: Why are you asking?

ELDEST: You owe him your freedom.

CORRUPT: The Sodomites defend us because they fear us.
                They know deep in their hearts that we will
                destroy Sodom. But when the day of judgement
                comes, we will show no mercy. Everyone will be
                slaughtered except for the young children, the
                beautiful women, and those who have served us.

ELDEST: Do you want to kill my father?

CORRUPT: Let's not talk about it. If I don't kill him,
                someone else will. When we have to, we kill our
                own.

ELDEST: Maybe your Leader has made a mistake.

CORRUPT: The Leader never makes mistakes. The earth can
                always soaks up more blood —doesn't matter

whose blood it is. That's what our prophet teaches.

ELDEST: I just can't agree with that.

CORRUPT: Because Lot is your father. He pretends to be a Sodomite but he talks like Abraham. We'll soon wipe out both. When we're done with Sodom, we'll go after Canaan and Mamre.

ELDEST: One day someone might wipe you out.

CORRUPT: Gomorrah will stand forever.

YOUNGEST and OAF enter.

YOUNGEST: Hey! You're here?

ELDEST: Are we in your way?

YOUNGEST: No, but Oaf wants to teach me how to dance.

ELDEST: Dance as much as you want.

YOUNGEST: He's teaching Bitchy to dance.

ELDEST: Really?

OAF: I go to her place every day.

ELDEST: Do you think she beheaded Looter?

OAF: Someone beheaded him.

ELDEST: It's the only thing people are talking about. Our mother wanted to invite both sisters for dinner, but they're booked for the next three months.

YOUNGEST: People will soon forget. That's how it is: we make a fuss about someone, and soon forget them. Other girls also have lovers and they can chop off heads too.

CORRUPT: In Sodomite temples, all you talk about is mercy, love, kindness, and stuff like that. But when a woman brings her lover to justice, everyone gets down on their knees.

YOUNGEST: Don't people murder in Gomorrah?

CORRUPT: More than they do here, but they don't make so much noise about it.

YOUNGEST: Come, Oaf, I'm tired of all this talk. My sister follows in my father's footsteps – arguing with everybody. But I think young women should just be pretty, play the harp, sing, dance, and know the secrets of love. The men will take care of the rest.

CORRUPT: That's the kind of thing a Sodom girl would say.

YOUNGEST: And what kinds of things do the girls say in Gomorrah?

CORRUPT: Girls in Gomorrah are just like the men. They're concerned with the well-being of the country.

They work for the government as much as the
men.

YOUNGEST: They're slaves, we're masters. Which is better?

CORRUPT: You won't stay masters for long.

YOUNGEST: The young and beautiful always stick around.
               Come, Oaf, let's dance.

OAF: Let's go. *(They dance)*

*LOT'S WIFE enters. She's followed by MAID. She carries a large
basket on her head and holds two water skeins.*

LOT'S WIFE: I'm tired. Put the things down. You're falling
               over – as if you were as burdened like a donkey.

MAID: I'll take the things inside. *(Leaves)*

ELDEST: Mother, this is Corrupt.

LOT'S WIFE: My daughter has told me so much about you. She
               described you as better-looking. But that's young
               women for you.

ELDEST: I was praising his mind, not his beauty.

LOT'S WIFE: Stop dancing. I'm tired. I found a bunch of
               bargains at the market, but they were no bargains
               at all. When Lot hears how much I've spent, he'll
               start yelling.

CORRUPT: Everyone in Sodom loves a bargain. We know better in Gomorrah. We're building a wall around the city, digging trenches, canals, forging swords, spears, axes, preparing to set our enemies on fire. Gomorrah's sages only think about one thing: how to subjugate those who don't yet know the truth.

LOT'S WIFE: If you like Gomorrah so much, what are you doing in Sodom?

CORRUPT: It's better here for now. But how long will it last? My motto is: take what you can from Sodom – then stick a knife in its back. Sodom's like an old cow: first you milk it, then you slaughter it. Sodom's like a good dream – and soon it'll be time to wake up.

LOT'S WIFE: Wake up to what?

CORRUPT: Destruction.

LOT'S WIFE: All anyone talks about is destruction. What's making everyone so crazy? When I was a little girl, no one talked like this. All you hear is: destruction, destruction, destruction. Why should Sodom be destroyed?

ELDEST: Because it's built on contradictions.

LOT'S WIFE: I don't know what you're talking about.

YOUNGEST: She doesn't know either. She's just repeating whatever Corrupt says.

LOT'S WIFE: What kind of contradictions?

BASTARD enters.

BASTARD: Hello, everyone.

LOT'S WIFE: Bastard! *(She kisses him)* Where's Lot?

BASTARD: Lot's busy with Snitchy.

LOT'S WIFE: What business does he have with her?

BASTARD: Who can know what goes on between a woman
                 who chopped off her lover's head – and her
                 defense lawyer? I saw him go into her room and
                 she closed the door.

LOT'S WIFE: And how did you happen to see this?

BASTARD: I was passing by.

LOT'S WIFE: Snitchy's house isn't on your way home.

BASTARD: I was thinking about the verdict and my feet
                 carried me to her house. I walked by, heard Lot's
                 voice, and peeked in through the keyhole.

OAF: I peeked through the keyhole too.

BASTARD: Who's he?

LOT'S WIFE: *(To OAF)* What are you doing here?

YOUNGEST: He's teaching Bitchy to dance.

LOT'S WIFE: Why didn't you tell me that you saw my
                 husband?

OAF: I only gossip for pay.

CORRUPT: Everything is Sodom is about money. In
                 Gomorrah, children learn gossip and denunciation
                 in school, and only the kind that's useful for the
                 state.

BASTARD: Who are you?

CORRUPT: Earlier today, Judge, you freed me from a false
                 accusation.

BASTARD: The guy who likes Gomorrah?

CORRUPT: The guy who loves the people.

BASTARD: What are you doing here?

ELDEST: He's my friend.

BASTARD: Does your father know?

LOT'S WIFE: Back in my day, a girl's parents chose her husband
                 and got a bride price for their daughter. Lot paid
                 four hundred shekels and eight oxen for me. But
                 young women today do whatever they like.

ELDEST: The old days are gone.

LOT'S WIFE: We were one of the first families in Sodom, and
                your father was a foreigner who came from Ur of
                the Chaldees. He came from a family whose name
                I'd rather not mention – and people could hardly
                even understand when he spoke Sodomese. But
                my blessed father was there when he defended a
                thief in court, and he said: a young man who
                could find so many arguments on behalf of a thief
                would not fail in Sodom. He brought him home
                and they agreed on the price.

BASTARD: You should've heard how he defended Snitchy
                today. Her innocence rose to the surface like oil on
                water.

LOT'S WIFE: My husband's hired by the greatest thieves in
                Sodom. They ask his advice before they even
                commit the crime. So why not murderers?

BASTARD: You're telling me? It's gotten to the point that
                I'm afraid to walk down the street.

LOT'S WIFE: You're the one freeing them, not Lot.

BASTARD: The law's on their side.

CORRUPT: How long can such a city exist?

BASTARD: Are there no murderers in Gomorrah?

CORRUPT: The murderers in Gomorrah do what the Leader
                says. Every murder is commanded for a reason. In
                Sodom, it's just chaos.

GUZZLER enters.

BASTARD: Hey look, it's Guzzler.

LOT'S WIFE: Hello, Guzzler.

GUZZLER: Where's Lot?

LOT'S WIFE: Late.

GUZZLER: Held up by Snitchy.

LOT'S WIFE: How do you know? Were you there too?

GUZZLER: Passing by.

LOT'S WIFE: At least Lot can tell a good lie.

GUZZLER: I'm tired.

BASTARD: *(to GUZZLER)* Do you know this young man?

GUZZLER: Yes, the guy who loves Gomorrah.

BASTARD: He's Eldest's friend.

GUZZLER: I wouldn't be surprised if you told me that he
                  visits the king's palace on a regular basis.

CORRUPT: I once taught Princess Nasty.

GUZZLER: This city indulges anyone who wants to see it
                  ruined.

ELDEST: Sodom is built on contradictions.

LOT enters.

LOT: My friends! My dear wife! I have a gift for you.
                  (Kisses her)

ELDEST: Papa!

YOUNGEST: Daddy! *(They kiss him)*

LOT'S WIFE: Why so late?

LOT: I had a tough day. First the trial of that murderess
                  Snitchy. Then I had to defend a traitor to our
                  country. And then. . .

LOT'S WIFE: And then what happened?

LOT: I had to look up an old law and I went to consult
                  the old parchments. It took me a long time to
                  find what I needed.

LOT'S WIFE: Did the parchments smell of perfume?

LOT: I don't know what you're talking about.

LOT'S WIFE: You smell of ointment and salve.

LOT: That's from the saleswoman who sold me your
                  gift.

LOT'S WIFE: Did you find what you were looking for in the
                  parchment?

LOT: Yes and no, but you have to look for it anyway.

LOT'S WIFE: Your parchments have very long hair. *(Plucks a hair from his clothes)*

LOT: It's the saleswoman. Hello, judge, and hello to you, Guzzler. Here's your gift, darling. *(Gives his wife a string of pearls)*

LOT'S WIFE: Beautiful!

ELDEST: And so expensive!

YOUNGEST: What did you bring me, daddy?

LOT: I have something for both of you. Who's this young man? He looks familiar.

CORRUPT: You just defended me today, sir.

LOT: Corrupt! What are you doing here?

LOT'S WIFE: He's an acquaintance of our eldest.

LOT: What?

ELDEST: He's my friend.

LOT: Since when?

ELDEST: A while.

LOT: Did I know about this?

LOT'S WIFE: He taught Princess Nasty.

LOT: Welcoming guests is Sodom's greatest tradition.
                But –

CORRUPT: But what?

LOT: I'm a little drunk and so I'll tell you something
                that I might not have said otherwise.

LOT'S WIFE: Better not.

LOT: Every day I defend thieves, murderers, liars,
                cheats, all kinds of rebels. But I wouldn't want
                any of them to get close to my daughter.

CORRUPT: But today, sir, you told me that –

LOT: What I say in court and what I say at home are
                two different things.

ELDEST: The eternal hypocrisy of Sodom.

LOT: I thought that you were a chaste young woman
                with good sense and a modest heart. Now I see
                what road you've chosen.

ELDEST: I'm no longer the little girl who sat upon your
                knee.

YOUNGEST: I'm not a child anymore either.

LOT: What's going on? Am I in Sodom or Gomorrah?

BASTARD: There isn't as much difference as we think.

LOT: I'll rule my house as I see fit. My daughters will
                 not run around with debauchers.

YOUNGEST: Too late.

ELDEST: Are you blind, or are you pretending? Your
                 daughters are no better than any other young
                 women in Sodom.

YOUNGEST: Maybe even a little worse.

LOT: So all my hard work was for nothing. I defended
                 murderers, thieves, and robbers – all for you. I
                 racked my brain to find a defense for every
                 criminal so that you two would have everything
                 you needed so that you could marry the best
                 young men in Sodom. You're right: I was blind. I
                 worked so hard – only to raise two Sodomite
                 whores.

LOT'S WIFE: What are you talking about? You're drunk.

LOT: I speak the truth. It took me years to build
                 everything – but I could destroy it in an hour.

ELDEST: Like your uncle Abraham who shattered all his
                 father's idols?

LOT'S WIFE: Don't speak to your father that way.

YOUNGEST: She's right. In his heart he's a Hebrew – not a Sodomite.

LOT'S WIFE: You're embarrassing me in front of our guests.

LOT: They say the same thing. They belittle me every day.

BASTARD: You are what you are, but we don't think you're a fool. What did you think? That in the middle of Sodom you could maintain a Hebrew home? Your daughters go out, they have friends, they see how other young women behave.

GUZZLER: How can you expect modesty from your daughters when you spend your days with parchment that wears perfume and has long hair?

LOT: Get out of my house! All of you go to hell!

LOT'S WIFE: What's wrong with you?

LOT: You're right. I act like everyone else in Sodom. But I can still tell the difference between good and evil. I defend murderers, but I hate blood. I'm an adulterer, but I don't want my wife and daughters spending time with –

GUZZLER: Shut up!

BASTARD: You're not one of us. We let you become rich. We let you marry into one of our most prominent families. We made you the senior defense attorney, even though you're a foreigner who still can't speak Sodomese fluently. But if you can't forget where you came from – we'll take it all away. We'll put you on trial, and this time your clever tongue won't help you.

LOT'S WIFE: Lot, you can't stand with one foot in Sodom and the other in Mamre. The parchment you looked at today is called Snitchy. You can't fool me as well as I can fool you.

LOT: Have you been cheating on me?

LOT'S WIFE: Behind all your pretty words and big ideas, you're a simpleton.

LOT: You slept with someone else? I'll kill you all, and then I'll kill myself.

LOT'S WIFE: Look at him! Now he's jealous!

BASTARD: You have two sets of rules. Our wives and daughters can be disgraced. But your wife and your daughters are holy lambs.

LOT: I'm not the one who corrupted Sodom. When I first came here, you were already up to your necks in injustice.

BASTARD: So why did you stay?

GUZZLER: Because evil is bad, but his wife, and daughters, and money are all very good.

CORRUPT: I've heard enough. I'm leaving.

ELDEST: Where are you going? Wait!

CORRUPT: I'm not wanted here, but let me tell you, Lot, that
                 of all the fools, you're the biggest. I slept with
                 your daughter, and before I slept with her, she'd
                 already slept with someone else. You wife has
                 slept with Bastard, and Guzzler, and lots of other
                 Bastards and Guzzlers. While you're defending
                 adulterers in court, other adulterers are lying in
                 your bed with your wife and daughters.

LOT: Where's my sword? I'll chop off his head!

CORRUPT: I'm ready to fight you. Go – get your sword!

LOT'S WIFE: Get out of here! Go and never come back!

CORRUPT: Coward! *(Spits)*

ELDEST: I'm going with you!

CORRUPT: Leave me alone! *(Leaves)*

ELDEST: Mother! *(Weeps)*

LOT: Bastard, is this true? *(Turns)* Guzzler? *(Pause)*
                 Why are you all so quiet?

OAF: If you pay me, sir, I'll tell you everything.

LOT: Talk!

BASTARD: Get out of here, young man, or you'll be sent to
                 the gallows!

OAF: I was just kidding.

GUZZLER: You'll soon be a head shorter.

OAF: I'm leaving, I'm leaving.

YOUNGEST: I'm going with you!

OAF: Not now. *(Leaves)*

LOT: Well, it's all clear now. I'm leaving this place and all of you. *(Calls out)* Maid!

MAID: *(Enters)* Yes, my lord.

LOT: Go pack my clothes. Saddle my donkey. Make me some matzahs and a skein of water.

MAID: My lord's going away?

LOT'S WIFE: He's not going anywhere. He's drunk.

MAID: What should I do?

LOT'S WIFE: Go back to your chamber.

LOT: I'm your master. Do as I say.

LOT'S WIFE: Go back to your chamber. *(MAID leaves)*

LOT: You were right. Under the surface, I'm Sodom's biggest fool. Bastard, I will no longer defend anyone in court. I'll leave Sodom, if not by donkey, then on foot.

GUZZLER: You don't know how to drink.

LOT: I don't know how to live. That's the truth. I also
                don't know how to die.

LOT'S WIFE: Where will you go? There's no other place for
                someone like you.

LOT: If there was a place for Cain, there'll be
                somewhere for me.

BASTARD: Really, Lot, I don't understand you.

LOT: For thirty years, all I wanted was to become one of
                you. I wanted to find some meaning in your
                madness. Like an ape, I did what you did. Like a
                parrot, I said what you said. I wanted people to
                see me as more of a Sodomite than anyone else,
                and they did. But here's the truth: I could never
                get used to you. I never liked your holidays. I
                never laughed at your jokes. I'm still afraid of
                duels. Adam and Eve ate from the Tree of
                Knowledge and learned the difference between
                good and evil. But you come from the time when
                Adam and Eve went naked and did not know it.

GUZZLER: So why didn't you stay with Abraham?

LOT: I couldn't live with him either.

BASTARD: Why not?

LOT: He's too much of a Hebrew.

LOT'S WIFE: Who could you live with?

ELDEST: You spent a fortune on tutors. If we ever used a
                   Hebrew word, you'd tell us we were debasing the
                   Sodomese language. All of a sudden, Sodom is
                   worthless –

LOT: I wanted you to learn the good things that Sodom
                   had to offer, not the bad.

YOUNGEST: What's there to learn in Sodom? How to murder,
                   how to cheat, how to sleep with men and steal
                   their money.

LOT: You're right. I drove you to this kind of
                   prostitution.

LOT'S WIFE: You were once a stranger – and you'll always be a
                   stranger. What you call prostitution we call love,
                   and what you call murder is a game to us. You
                   should know this by now.

MAID: *(Entering)* There are guests. They want to come
                   in.

LOT: What guests? My wife's lovers?

MAID: They're not from around here. They're dressed
                   like Canaanites.

LOT: What do they look like?

MAID: White beards and long robes.

LOT: Why didn't you ask for their names?

MAID: I'll ask. *(Leaves)*

LOT'S WIFE: Could it be your family?

MAID: *(Returning)* One of them is named Abraham. The other won't tell me his name.

LOT'S WIFE: Mazel tov, your uncle Abraham is here.

LOT: Impossible! *(Runs to meet them)*

LOT'S WIFE: Don't bring them here.

LOT: I'm still in charge around here! *(Exits)*

LOT'S WIFE: All these years, I always hoped he would become one of us. Now you all see my disgrace. I never told anyone what I put up with. He drove away my daughters' friends. He wanted me to cover my face with a veil like his aunt Sarah. All the other women in Sodom openly bring their lovers into their bedrooms, but I had to watch every word I said. Now he's bringing his uncle Abraham and another good-for-nothing who won't even tell us his name into my house. *(Weeps)*

BASTARD: You've got to get rid of him.

GUZZLER: You took the words right out of my mouth.

ELDEST: What are you talking about? He's my father!

YOUNGEST: I still love him.

BASTARD: Love and murder aren't mutually exclusive.
                 Snitchy loved Looter, but she still got rid of him.

ELDEST: What are you talking about? Kill our father? You
                 might as well kill us.

YOUNGEST: Anything but that! Mommy! *(Weeps)*

LOT'S WIFE: What are you crying about? He's not dead yet!
                 They're cowards, like all the Hebrews!

*LOT enters with ABRAHAM and another man. Both have long
hair, white beards, long robes, and are barefoot.*

ABRAHAM: Greetings. *(Nobody answers)*

LOT: This is my uncle Abraham and this is his friend.
                 What's your name?

FRIEND: Why are you asking?

LOT: Is it a secret?

FRIEND: Yes.

BASTARD: We're used to people having names.

FRIEND: I could call myself by any name and no one would
                 know if it were true or false. But I do not lie, and
                 I must conceal the truth.

BASTARD: You never lie?

FRIEND: Never.

BASTARD: That's a lie.

ABRAHAM: This man is no liar. Truth reigns where he comes
                 from.

GUZZLER: There's no such place.

LOT: Why make such a fuss about a name? This is my
                 wife, and these are my two daughters.

ABRAHAM: They look like Sodomite girls, but you can still
                 see their grandparents' spark in their eyes.

GUZZLER: I don't see any spark.

BASTARD: Where are you from? Canaan?

ABRAHAM: Yes, from Mamre.

BASTARD: How did you get here? Did you go through
                 Gomorrah?

ABRAHAM: We did.

GUZZLER: And no one stopped you?

ABRAHAM: Here we are.

LOT: The road is blocked by a wall and a canal, and
                 sentries guard the way. No living creature can
                 pass – except a bird.

FRIEND: We spent the night in Gomorrah and now we're
                   in Sodom.

GUZZLER: Where did you spend the night?

FRIEND: Where else? In the street.

LOT'S WIFE: Then why are your clothes clean?

LOT: Why are you interrogating our guests? Tonight
                   they'll sleep here. Maid, wash their feet.

MAID: I'm coming. . .

GUZZLER: What's going on in Gomorrah? Very few people
                   make it here from there.

FRIEND: The city is full of lies and injustice. The powerful
                   rule and the powerless work hard. They have
                   nothing – not even food.

ELDEST: And truth reigns where you come from?

FRIEND: Yes.

ELDEST: I've been told that in Gomorrah everyone is equal.

LOT: Who told you that? Corrupt?

FRIEND: In Gomorrah, the prisons are full. The police are
                   also the judges. Anyone who falls out of favor
                   with the authorities is woken up in the middle of
                   the night and taken to the hangman – or to the
                   salt graves at the Dead Sea.

LOT: When exactly did you see all of this? In one night
                in the street?

FRIEND: Yes.

MAID: If you please, sir. (Kneels and washes their feet)

LOT'S WIFE: As long as you're under my roof, you should eat.
                Would you like leavened bread or matzah?

FRIEND: Bring food for Abraham if you want. I don't eat.

LOT'S WIFE: Why not?

FRIEND: I'm not hungry.

LOT'S WIFE: After such a long journey? Did you eat so much in
                Gomorrah?

FRIEND: No.

LOT'S WIFE: Will you drink wine?

FRIEND: I don't drink wine.

LOT'S WIFE: Milk from our goats?

FRIEND: Not that either.

LOT'S WIFE: What, then? Water from the well?

FRIEND: I'm not thirsty.

LOT: What sort of person are you? Uncle Abraham, I'll
                tell the servants to bring you something to eat
                and drink. *(Leaves)*

LOT'S WIFE: What brought you here?

ABRAHAM: I came to see my brother's son and his daughters.

LOT'S WIFE: Is this your servant? *(pointing to the stranger)*

ABRAHAM: He's not my servant. I'm his servant.

LOT'S WIFE: Really?

ABRAHAM: Yes.

LOT'S WIFE: Who ever heard of a servant going to meet his
                relatives and his master accompanying him?
                Don't laugh at us, Abraham.

ABRAHAM: I'm not laughing.

LOT'S WIFE: How's Sarah?

ABRAHAM: She's pregnant.

LOT'S WIFE: What? How old is she?

ABRAHAM: Not much younger than I am.

LOT'S WIFE: And she's pregnant?

ABRAHAM: Yes.

LOT'S WIFE: And you still insist that you're not laughing at us?

FRIEND: Sarah also laughed when she was told she was expecting. But it was no joke.

BASTARD: Why travel so far to make fun of us?

FRIEND: We're not making fun of anyone.

LOT: *(Enters)* Here's wine. They'll bring food for you soon, Uncle Abraham.

LOT'S WIFE: Your Uncle Abraham just told us that your Aunt Sarah is pregnant.

LOT: What? *(Laughs)*

ABRAHAM: It's true.

LOT: Have you turned into a comedian in your old age?

FRIEND: Is anything impossible for God?

LOT: I've never heard of an old woman becoming pregnant.

FRIEND: You will soon see and hear many things that you have not yet seen or heard.

GUZZLER: Like what? Come on, Bastard, these people came to make fun of Sodom and confuse us with riddles. But we're not easily confused. We know there's no such thing as a miracle.

FRIEND: Don't your idols enact miracles?

BASTARD: In the temple, and when we leave, we know that
                   nature is the same as it's always been. If you don't
                   throw a stone, it doesn't fall. If you chop off a
                   head, it doesn't grow back. If you don't eat, you
                   starve, and if your wife or lover puts poison in
                   your food, your bowels burn. We all know that
                   young women get pregnant and that old women
                   are as barren as sand in the desert.

FRIEND: But whoever brings life to a young womb can also
                   bring life to an old womb.

GUZZLER: Who's that supposed to be?

ABRAHAM: People said the same thing in Gomorrah.

BASTARD: There they destroyed the temples, melted down
                   the idols into armor and spears, and burned the
                   ancient parchments. Here, we've preserved it all.

FRIEND: What's the use of temples and parchments when
                   there's no faith?

YOUNGEST: They think faith is for the young. That we should
                   believe things that make them laugh. I was
                   laughing at all their miracles by the time I was
                   eight. But I still had to go to temple and listen to
                   the preacher's stupid sermons.

ELDEST: Sodom is built on hypocrisy! At the temple they
                   kneel, bow, sacrifice to the gods. But in the street
                   they deny it all. In the courthouse, they blab

about truth and justice, but in the marketplace
they make fun of it all. Under the wedding
canopy, the bride swears fidelity, but the next day
she sleeps with someone else. That's why
Gomorrah will destroy us.

FRIEND: Why should your destruction come from
               Gomorrah? The people there are no better than
               you.

BASTARD: Destruction has to come from somewhere. It can't
               just come from the sky. *(Laughs)*

CURTAIN.

Scene 4

In front of LOT'S house. CORRUPT is giving a speech.

CORRUPT: It's clear what's next. Not only is Sodom
               exploiting its citizens, we're also preparing to
               launch war against Gomorrah. Why do our rulers
               impose high taxes? Because they need to prepare
               for war. But what will war bring us? The other
               side is ready too. They'll answer sword with
               sword, arrow with arrow, fire with fire. Theirs
               will be a just war. The tips of their spears are
               dipped in a new philosophy, a doctrine about the
               earth god, while we go to war for the sake of a few
               elites who suck the people dry like spiders. Sodom
               will be torn to pieces. And so --

CITIZEN 1:   Before you say anything else, let me ask
               something!

CORRUPT: Go ahead.

CITIZEN 1:   Have you ever lived in Gomorrah?

CORRUPT: No, but --

CITIZEN 1:   I spent many years there. I'm from Gomorrah and
                let me tell you, citizens of Sodom, they impose
                ten times the taxes that we do, and they spend a
                lot more on swords and spears. Their children are
                taught to use weapons. Their women learn to
                fight. They talk about destroying Sodom every
                day.

CORRUPT: So why did you leave Gomorrah?

CITIZEN 1:   Because I worked hard and never had enough to
                fill my belly. You know what I did? I made
                slingshots to crack Sodom's walls. Later, they
                made a false accusation against me, and put me in
                chains and made me work in shackles –

CORRUPT: They probably didn't do it for nothing.

CITIZEN 1:   – because I had the nerve to say that I was
                hungry – and my overseer gave away my food to
                one of his favorite prostitutes.

CORRUPT: It's clear as day, people, that this man is a traitor.
                Everyone from Gomorrah tells us that there are no
                prostitutes there and the overseers are all
                respectable people. Why would a woman need to
                be a prostitute if she can freely sleep with whoever

she wants and have plenty of food and her pick of clothes from the country's treasures? Why would the overseers steal when there's plenty for everyone?

CITIZEN 2:   Corrupt – don't bother with him. He's been paid off by Sodom's elites.

CITIZEN 3:   We should rip out his teeth and yank his tongue out of his throat.

CORRUPT: His time will come, brothers. The day of judgement is near.

WOMAN: Can I say something?

CORRUPT: Of course. In Sodom, women are treated worse than slaves. But in Gomorrah, men and women are both equally enslaved by the Leader.

WOMAN: Men in Sodom all kill each other while women either become spinsters or marry old men that no longer have fire in their loins. Pretty women are like goddesses and everyone else bows before them and lets them murder whoever they want. But when a woman is not so pretty and can't cover her flaws with makeup, she's worse than shit. Is this right? Should Sodom worship a few whores?

OLD MAN: And how are elders treated here? They give me a bit of bread but no one wants to talk to me or follow my advice. The elderly used to head the family, rule their tribe. Today there's no greater shame than being old. Everyone lies about their

age. Men and women both give away their last
pennies to dye their hair black and paint their
cheeks red so they look younger.

OLD WOMAN: Once upon a time, men would sleep with women.
Now it's rare. The best-looking young men in
Sodom only sleep with other men. What's left for
us?

WOMAN: All that's left is to follow their example.

CORRUPT: Everyone in Sodom has been wronged – young,
old, men, women. It's completely different in
Gomorrah. Our Leader takes care of each and
every one of us. Gomorrah has a Minister of
Matchmaking who issues orders about who should
sleep with whom. The elderly aren't idle, they
work for the state. In Gomorrah, nobody dyes
their hair –

CITIZEN 1:   Because they don't have enough money to buy
dye!

CITIZEN 2:   No, because they're doing useful work for the
good of the state!

CITIZEN 1:   My job was making poison for arrows. But what
was the point?

CORRUPT: What should they do, wait for Sodom to
annihilate them?

CITIZEN 1:   What should we do, sit with our hands folded and
wait for Gomorrah to annihilate us?

CORRUPT: You sit here like worms in horseradish with no
idea what's happening in the world. You don't
even know what's happening here. You see this
house? Who owns it? Lot. Did he build it? No, he
bought it. How? By defending murderers,
thieves, prostitutes, and con-men. He teaches
murderers how to murder in advance – and
thieves how to steal and go unpunished. Everyone
in Sodom knows that Snitchy cut off Looter's head
because she wanted another man, but they laid
the blame on Bitchy, who's already a murderer
and a whore. And who defended Snitchy? Lot.

CITIZEN 3: He's not even one of us. Real Sodomites go around
with torn clothes and empty stomachs, and that
Hebrew rides on a golden saddle.

CORRUPT: You're right! But that's not enough. Sodomites
like to use pretty words, but we have to turn our
words into actions.

CITIZEN 3: What should we do?

CORRUPT: Sabotage Sodom. We can't miss a single
opportunity to stab the swine in the back. When
the time is right, we'll take up our swords and our
torches – and set this place ablaze. Sodom is no
longer our homeland, but our greatest enemy.

CITIZEN 3: When will this happen? What are you waiting
for? You've been talking this way for years. I'm
ready!

CORRUPT: Your anger is justified, but there's no point in
                starting a rebellion if we can't finish it. We need
                to unite and wait, like soldiers, for orders from
                Gomorrah. When the Leader sees the time is
                right, he'll give us the signal.

CITIZEN 2:   I'm getting old. When the time comes, I may not
                have enough strength to kill anyone.

CORRUPT: There will be others. We have plenty of
                bloodthirsty people in Sodom.

OAF appears. He's carrying a drum and a picture of SNITCHY.

OAF: *(Drumming)* This is the great Snitchy. She is no
                mere woman but a goddess. She's had eight men
                and none of them died a natural death. She's had
                more lovers than strands of hair on her head. She
                has 48 pairs of shoes, 32 coats, 80 velvet shirts,
                and 72 –

CORRUPT: Can't you find another place to pay homage to
                Snitchy? Or did the elites pay you to disturb me?

OAF: You're paid for what you say, I'm paid for what I
                say. You need to live, I need to live. Sodomites!
                Do you know what Snitchy uses for her daily
                bath? A bathtub full of balsam. She keeps a vial of
                oils from Ethiopia between her breasts.
                Hairdressers visit her morning and night,
                arranging her hair – black as pitch and as soft as
                velvet. She uses eight different colors to adorn her
                godly face, which shines like the sun at noon. Her

nails are sharp as spears and red as glowing coals.
Her breasts –

CORRUPT: Are you done?

WOMAN: What's happened to the men around here? Have
                they all lost their minds? Have they never seen a
                pair of breasts? I have breasts too – no one's
                looking at them!

OAF: Pay me and I'll praise your breasts too.

OLD WOMAN: Where are we supposed to get money if we don't
                have enough for food? Snitchy gets hundreds of
                shekels for spending the night with a man while
                people like me can't even get a man for free. The
                adulation, the ballads, the pictures – it just makes
                me jealous. I go to sleep hungry for food and
                thirsty for men, and I don't even know what hurts
                more, the hunger in my belly or the thirst in my
                blood.

OAF: Pay me. I'll find you a man.

CORRUPT: There are no women in Gomorrah like Snitchy,
                and nobody carries their pictures. The town criers
                carry pictures of the Leader and his ministers, the
                people's defenders. Everyone praises them and
                everyone bows down to them.

CITIZEN 1:   We bow before our gods.

CORRUPT: Our gods are clay and stone. They can't do
                anything. We pour wine on their heads, but if we
                poured piss, they would like it just as much. But
                Gomorrah's Leader is a living god, a wrathful god,
                a god of might, a god who takes vengeance on his
                enemies and destroys anyone who dares to rebel
                against his word. He also rewards those who
                worship him and sing his praises day and night.
                Isn't it better to serve a god like this than a god
                that can't even move?

ABRAHAM enters. LOT runs after him and tries to hold him back.

VOICES: Who's this?

CORRUPT: Lot's guest. A spy from Canaan.

LOT: I'm begging you, Abraham, don't get involved in
                their arguments. Please, come home.

ABRAHAM: My friend, my master, urged me to speak to them.
                I tried to tell them in Gomorrah, and I must try
                to be heard here.

CORRUPT: What do you want to say – Lot's uncle, Canaanite
                spy? And where did you leave that friend of yours
                who doesn't even have a name – like a bastard?

ABRAHAM: It's true that I come from Canaan, but I'm no spy.
                I'm a stranger there too.

VOICE 1:   Then go back to where you came from.

VOICE 2:   Go to hell.

ABRAHAM: Patience, my brother. I'm an old man, my time in
                Sodom is short. Every word I say to you comes
                from God. Ten generations ago, our ancestors
                sinned, filling the earth with thievery and
                murder. God brought on a flood that washed
                everything away. Only righteous Noah and his
                household remained. You should know that what
                went on in the time of the flood is still happening
                today. The Almighty promised not to bring on
                any more floods of water, but he can still bring a
                flood of fire.

CORRUPT: Are you the same Abraham who destroyed his
                father's gods and then ran away to Canaan?

ABRAHAM: I am.

CORRUPT: How can you speak in the name of God when you
                go around destroying other people's gods?

ABRAHAM: I destroyed idols that were molded from clay,
                carved from wood, cut from stone. I speak in the
                name of the God who created the heavens and the
                earth and the sea and the desert and the sun and
                the moon and the stars and all of the people and
                animals and birds, the God who loves justice.

VOICE 1:   He's crazy.

VOICE 2:   There's no such god!

CORRUPT: Where is this god? Where does he live? Which
                palace?

ABRAHAM: How can he live in a palace when even the
                heavens and the four corners of the earth are too
                small for him? He is the God who created Adam
                and Noah and who brought on the flood, and who
                will also destroy Sodom if you don't repent.

CORRUPT: A spy disguised as a madman.

ABRAHAM: You speak only about who will destroy whom –
                Sodom or Gomorrah. But it is God's wish to
                destroy both. Neither of you believes in the
                creator, but only in the strength of arm and horse,
                shield and chariot. Who are your heroes?
                Murderers and whores. Your courts are full of
                injustice. Your judges take bribes. Your writers
                write of blood and lechery. Your poets sing of
                murder and debauchery. Half your earnings are
                spent on wine, beer, whores, sorcery, gambling,
                and fights. You speak of charity, but your poor are
                naked and barefoot. You speak of love but your
                every breath is full of hate. You hate the people of
                Gomorrah and you hate each other. Snitchy
                chopped off her lover's head – and Sodom can't
                stop singing about her. You have more respect for
                a bloody knife than for the wisdom of the sages.

CORRUPT: Is Lot any better?

ABRAHAM: No.

LOT: Don't argue with them. They're the scum of
                Sodom.

ABRAHAM: All of Sodom is scum.

CORRUPT: How much did Lot pay you for this speech? How
                much silver did you get from Canaan to shame
                and spit upon the good people of Sodom? We
                Sodomites have seen a lot of prophets – and
                they've all been paid off.

ABRAHAM: Nobody paid me.

VOICE 1:   Then your words are worthless.

ABRAHAM: I came to warn you that God intends to destroy
                Sodom. It could happen sooner than you think.

VOICE 1:   What do you want us to do?

ABRAHAM: Repent.

VOICE 1:   What's that?

ABRAHAM: Be ashamed of your transgressions and promise
                never to sin again.

CORRUPT: What sins? What's the old fool blabbing about?

ABRAHAM: God's word is clear: do not steal, do not murder,
                do not bear false witness. Judge fairly, help the
                poor and the sick, do not commit adultery, do not
                embarrass anyone, do not ruin someone's

reputation. Do not worship idols and do not
sacrifice your children to them –

VOICE 1:   Why are you telling us this? We're not Sodom's
                elites.

ABRAHAM: You are the people of Sodom.

VOICE 1:   Sodom would be no better with our penitence.

ABRAHAM: Someone has to start.

VOICE 1:   Why me?

ABRAHAM: God promised me that if there were just ten
                righteous people in Sodom, he would protect the
                city for their sake.

CORRUPT: Empty words. One person can't make a difference.
                Even a hundred or five hundred people can't
                change the culture. There's only one way: take the
                wealth away from the rich and give it all to a
                Leader who can divide it according to what
                everyone needs and what they've earned.

ABRAHAM: A wicked ruler divides wickedly.

CORRUPT: We'll make sure he divides it fairly.

ABRAHAM: Who? If people don't want to repent, those who
                watch will steal and divide their plunder amongst
                themselves.

CORRUPT: Then the people will rise up and kill them.

ABRAHAM: Without penitence, without faith in God and his
                justice, no ruler will ever be good. I was in
                Gomorrah and I saw their Leader: he is an evil
                man who sheds the blood of innocents.

CORRUPT: He's evil and you're a saint? You'll pay dearly for
                these words, Abraham. You'll rot in jail. You'll be
                rent limb from limb and the dogs will eat your
                flesh. Our Leader has spies everywhere and his
                arm is long enough to punish you even in Canaan
                or in Egypt. You're crazy. How do people even
                repent? How does it help anybody?

ABRAHAM: When you body gets dirty, you wash it and it gets
                clean. It's the same with the soul. If it gets
                polluted, it must be purified. How do you purify
                a soul? With repentance, thinking about your
                deeds and weighing them on the scale of good and
                evil, praying to God and promising to follow the
                righteous path. A city can only be pure when its
                citizens remove their personal waste. Everyone
                must do this for themselves.

CORRUPT: People – how long will you keep listening to this
                old fool?

VOICE 1:   Drive him away!

VOICE 2:   Send him back to Canaan!

YOUNG GIRL: I don't need penitence, I need a husband.

WOMAN: You can't eat repentance!

ABRAHAM: If you do not repent, it will be your downfall! I'm
                  telling you this because I pity you.

Someone throws a stone. Suddenly, there are stones from all sides.

LOT: What are you doing?

CORRUPT: Kill him!

*They start throwing stones at LOT, but he runs back inside the
house. ABRAHAM follows him.*

CORRUPT: Break down the door.

OAF: Let's wait. Snitchy's breasts are like two skeins of
                  wine and blood. He who lies upon her bosom dies
                  of joy. . .

*His voice is drowned out by the crowd. The door opens and we see
ABRAHAM'S FRIEND.*

FRIEND: Why are you knocking on the door? What are you
                  screaming about?

VOICE: Who's this idiot?

CORRUPT: Lot's guest.

VOICES: Tear out his beard! Shatter his teeth! Hang him!

YOUNG GIRL: Castrate him!

FRIEND: What have I done to you?

CORRUPT: We have enough lunatics in Sodom. We don't
need foreign ones.

OAF: I can't worship Snitchy because of you!

FRIEND: Only to the Creator of heaven and earth should be
worshipped.

OAF: I get paid by Snitchy, not the Creator.

FRIEND: You're all blind. You are like your laws: you have
eyes but do not see. You have ears but do not hear.
God's voice calls to you every day: turn towards it!
God did not create humanity for murder and
theft. He molded you in his image. He gave you
knowledge so that you would choose the
righteous path and avoid evil. You know what
happened to your ancestors in the time of the
flood –

CORRUPT: That again? *(Throws a stone at him)*

FRIEND: Sodomites – you've gone blind. If Abraham
hadn't pleaded for you day and night, there'd be
nothing left of you.

CORRUPT: We'll soon see who's blind! (grabs a spear) Hold
him, I'll pluck out his eyes!

FRIEND: Do I deserve this?

VOICES: Hold him! Hold him!

FRIEND: You're blind! Blind!

VOICE 1:   I can't see anything!

VOICE 2:   I'm blind!

CORRUPT: He made us blind!

YOUNG GIRL: How?

OAF: With poison.

FRIEND: Not with poison. With the word of God.

WOMAN: Can we still repent?

FRIEND: Yes.

CORRUPT: Don't talk to him. He blinded you and he'll kill
                you too. We'll go to the judges and tell them
                what Lot's spies have done to us!

VOICE 1:   I can't see the way!

CORRUPT: I'll lead you. Take each other by the hand.

OAF: Snitchy's picture! I lost it!

FRIEND: I'm warning you: repent and God will put the
                light back in your eyes!

CORRUPT: Quiet, you old dog! You'll be hung tonight...

CORRUPT leads them away in a line. Curtain.

ACT II

Scene 1

LOT's garden, late at night. LOT, ABRAHAM, and the FRIEND.

LOT: I don't understand anything, Uncle Abraham.

ABRAHAM: What don't you understand?

LOT: All of it. Assuming your God really exists – why did he make all this? He makes birth, he brings death. He builds, he destroys. Ten generations ago there was a flood. Now you say there'll be a flood of fire. Is that justice? Is it mercy?

FRIEND: God hates injustice.

LOT: If he hates injustice so much, he should not allow the unjust to emerge from their mothers' wombs. First he lets them commit injustices, then he punishes them for it?

FRIEND: He wants humanity to choose between good and evil.

LOT: People will never choose good.

FRIEND: Abraham's a person – and he's chosen good.

ABRAHAM: I am but dust and ashes.

LOT: There's a saying in Sodom: one bird does not a summer make.

FRIEND: Humanity must learn everything on its own. How
                   did people discover that the earth can give bread?
                   They saw a stalk of wheat in the field and tried to
                   plant its seed – waiting to see what would appear.
                   How do they know that bile is bitter? They tasted
                   it upon their lips. They learned things the hard
                   way: that snakes are poisonous even after they've
                   been beheaded, that fire burns, that wine
                   intoxicates, that bread is filling, that water is
                   refreshing, that wool is warm. And that's how
                   they will learn justice.

LOT: They will never learn.

FRIEND: They'll have no choice. This is their fate. Those
                   who don't learn will die.

LOT: And good people will never die?

FRIEND: Should people stop plowing and planting because
                   of locusts, storms, and droughts? People do what
                   they do – year in, year out – and the rest is up to
                   God.

LOT: I'd laugh – if I hadn't seen you make those people
                   blind.

FRIEND: God protects those who believe in Him, not those
                   who need Him to work wonders.

LOT'S WIFE appears.

LOT'S WIFE: It's late. Lot, come to bed.

LOT: I'm coming.

FRIEND: Tomorrow morning Sodom will be destroyed.

LOT: Tomorrow?

FRIEND: Tomorrow.

LOT;   What should I do?

FRIEND: You and your family don't deserve to be protected
                    – but Abraham has interceded on your behalf.
                    Gather your belongings and get ready to flee
                    tomorrow at the first light of dawn.

LOT: I have too much to gather overnight.

FRIEND: You have one night.

LOT'S WIFE: What are you talking about? Since you two
                    arrived there's been no peace around here. They
                    want to hang us and burn us and tear us to pieces.
                    I don't believe you, old man.

LOT: Don't say that, my dear. You didn't see what I
                    saw.

LOT'S WIFE: I didn't see it and I don't believe it. It's a warm
                    evening. The sky is clear. A nightingale is
                    singing. Where's this destruction coming from?
                    Ridiculous!

ELDEST: *(Appearing at the door)* Mother!

LOT'S WIFE: Why aren't you sleeping? It's late!

ELDEST:`I woke up.

LOT'S WIFE: Why?

ELDEST: I was dreaming of Corrupt. I opened my eyes and
                   he wasn't there. I miss him so much – it's killing
                   me.

LOT: How are you not ashamed before Uncle Abraham?

LOT'S WIFE: There's no shame in Sodom.

FRIEND: Only animals feel no shame. Where there's no
                   shame, there's no fear of God.

LOT'S WIFE: You're so old-fashioned. Our grandmothers were
                   ashamed of everything. Today, everything's
                   uncovered – our flesh and our thoughts – that's
                   why we're so healthy.

FRIEND: You're not healthy. Sodom is sick – like someone
                   about to die.

ELDEST: I'm not sick, old man, I'm not! Just try me! You'll
                   be on the ground in a minute – I'll tear your
                   beard out!

LOT: That's how girls in Sodom speak.

FRIEND: I don't want to fight you.

ELDEST: So you're afraid of me?

LOT: He says that tomorrow morning Sodom will be
                destroyed. We have to be ready to leave.

ELDEST: Tomorrow morning? You're sure it's not a little
                later? *(Laughs loudly)*

YOUNGEST: *(Runs in, wrapped in a sheet)* Why are you all
                laughing? You woke me up. Oh, mama, I had a
                sweet dream. Oaf was with me. We were both
                naked and –

LOT: Enough! You're not alone.

ELDEST: This old man is saying that women should be
                ashamed and that Sodom is going to be destroyed
                tomorrow morning. (Laughs)

YOUNGEST: You come to us from Canaan with your foolish
                beliefs and foolish words. You embarrass us in
                front of our neighbors. Oaf left because of you.
                Father, if these people stay, I'm leaving.

ELDEST: Me too.

LOT: You're embarrassing me. We're known for our
                hospitality.

ELDEST: We're known for a lot of things. I don't want
                these people in our house!

ABRAHAM: How can you speak this way? Your aunts Milka
                and Yiska wouldn't believe their ears if they heard
                you.

YOUNGEST: Who cares about Auntie Milka and Auntie Yiska?
                 Why did you come here with all these stories
                 about all these aunts? We don't know them and
                 we don't want to know them.

ABRAHAM: They're your flesh and blood. Thanks to them and
                 to me God will protect you tomorrow morning
                 from fire and brimstone.

LOT'S WIFE: Sure, fire and brimstone. Go to sleep, children.
                 Come to bed, Lot.

LOT: I'm going to stay a little longer.

LOT'S WIFE: Come, children. Bastard and Guzzler were right.
                 (All three leave)

FRIEND: Well?

LOT: Is Sodom really going to be destroyed?

FRIEND: You heard me.

LOT: I thought you might be joking.

FRIEND: I don't joke.

LOT: It's hard to believe. Everything's so quiet. The
                 crickets are asleep. So is the nightingale. You can
                 hear the grass grow. This does not look like
                 destruction.

FRIEND: How many times have you experienced
                 destruction?

LOT: When daylight comes and people see I've packed
            my things, they'll think I'm crazy.

FRIEND: They won't have time to see you – or think about
            you.

LOT: My own family will laugh at me.

ABRAHAM: People laughed at Noah too when he built his ark.

LOT: *(Looks around. Looks at the sky)* It's hard to
            believe. *(Leaves)*

Long pause.

ABRAHAM: Maybe there are still ten righteous people in
            Sodom? Maybe it's not too late to warn them?

FRIEND: Too late, Abraham. Midnight has already come.
            The sentence is sealed.

ABRAHAM: May your servant not feel your wrath, but I'd like
            to go and talk to the people again. Maybe
            someone will repent? Maybe someone will, at the
            last moment, avoid God's punishment? I know
            how hard it is to be human.

FRIEND: Why go anywhere? I'll open your eyes and you'll
            see everything you want to see.

ABRAHAM: Will I be able to talk to them?

FRIEND: If they want to, they'll hear you.

ABRAHAM: What will I see?

FRIEND: A prison in Gomorrah.

*It grows dark. On a bundle of straw sits BACKSTABBER in chains.
On other bundles of straw sit CORRUPT, OAF, and all the others
who were made blind near LOT's house.*

WOMAN: I still don't understand. Where are we? What do
                they want with us?

CORRUPT: I keep telling you. Instead of turning right, we
                turned left, and crossed the border into
                Gomorrah. The guards have put us in jail. They
                think we're spies, or that we're trying to attack
                them. But when the officer comes and I tell him
                everything – about how those spies from Canaan
                blinded us while I praised Gomorrah. They'll free
                us right away – maybe reward us. Maybe they'll
                even be able to heal our blindness. (Taps his eyes)
                There's no wound.

OLD WOMAN: Will they let us go back to Sodom?

CORRUPT: No. But why would we want to go back? Sodom
                is going to be destroyed. Gomorrah will live and
                prosper.

OAF: It's all your fault. If you hadn't made your stupid
                speech, nothing would have happened.

CITIZEN 1:   And instead of leading us home, you dragged us
                to Gomorrah.

CORRUPT: I thought I was going the right way.

CITIZEN 2:   I have a wife and children. They won't know
                  where I went.

CITIZEN 3:   You're so poor, your wife won't miss you. She'll
                  find someone else to sleep with.

CITIZEN 2:   Scoundrel! *(He tries to hit him, but encounters
                  OAF instead)*

OAF: Hey! Watch who you're hitting! I'll knock you all
                  down.

WOMAN: This is terrible. How could I have known that
                  listening to your speech would lead to such
                  misery?

CORRUPT: Stop complaining. In Sodom, you would have
                  ended up a poor old maid, and when the
                  destruction came, nobody would've protected you.
                  Soldiers wouldn't even sleep with you. At least
                  here you'll get work – and someone may sleep
                  with you too.

OLD WOMAN: Who?

CORRUPT: The head matchmaker makes sure that every
                  woman gets a man of her own, because Gomorrah
                  wants its population to grow. Gomorrah wants
                  enough soldiers to conquer everything from
                  Sodom to India to Ethiopia to China.

OLD WOMAN: I have a brother in Sodom. I have a sister, I have a
              home. I want to go back!

CORRUPT: No one in Gomorrah cares that you're crying.

OAF: Someone should kill you. What's going to happen
              to me here?

CORRUPT: We need drummers here too. But instead of going
              around singing about that whore Snitchy, you'll
              sing about our Leader and proclaim his greatness
              to the people.

OAF: I can also dance

CORRUPT: We need dancers too. You'll dance for the Leader
              and praise his great deeds.

OAF: But I'm blind.

WOMAN: Dance with your feet, not your eyes.

OAF: I miss Bitchy. She promised she'd kill her sister
              and marry me.

CORRUPT: She'll have to find someone else.

OAF: She loves me – and I love her.

CORRUPT: In Sodom, people talk all day and night about
              love. They say that love comes from the gods, but
              in Gomorrah, we know that love comes from the
              earth. Love is nothing more than the heat emitted

by the swamps at night after the sun warms them all day.

CITIZEN 1:   You know everything.

CORRUPT: Our Leader wrote a great book. It has all the answers.

CITIZEN 2:   Doesn't the Leader of Gomorrah make mistakes?

CORRUPT: What are you talking about? They'll behead you for even thinking that the Leader could make a mistake.

CITIZEN 1:   Even gods make mistakes.

CORRUPT: Don't think I forgot all the things you said about Gomorrah. I'll tell them – they'll know how to handle you.

CITIZEN 2:   I only said good things about Gomorrah.

CITIZEN 3:   I cursed Sodom.

CORRUPT: I remember everything – and I'll pass it along. Gomorrah knows how to reward its friends and punish its enemies.

CITIZEN 1:   I know Gomorrah better than you do. I'm the only one who understands that when we crossed the border – I said goodbye to life. I only have one head and they will cut it off. In Gomorrah, it's better to be dead than alive.

CORRUPT: Listen to what he's saying. Every word will lead to
                  his downfall.

WOMAN: We hear – and will bear witness.

YOUNG GIRL: I hope that you'll only say good things about me,
                  Corrupt.

CORRUPT: I'll say what I know.

YOUNG GIRL: What do you know about us?

CORRUPT: I know enough. Everyone here knows everything
                  about each other. They have a book as big as a
                  spruce tree with everyone's name in it, and what
                  you've done – if you're a friend or an enemy, if
                  you're serve or harm the Leader. When someone
                  falls into our hands, we look them up in the book.

CITIZEN 1:   I've always hated Sodom. If you remember, at
                  Lot's house, I threw the first stone.

CITIZEN 2:   No, I threw the first stone.

CITIZEN 3:   You're a liar. I threw the first stone and I'm not
                  even sure if you threw the second.

CITIZEN 2:   Soon you'll be saying I didn't throw any stones at
                  all

CITIZEN 3:   I don't remember you throwing stones.

CITIZEN 2:   Corrupt, did I throw stones – or not?

CORRUPT: I'll answer, but only to the investigator.

CITIZEN 1:   Meanwhile, you're sitting on the same sprigs of
                straw as we are.

CORRUPT: I'm sitting on straw now, but tomorrow I'll be an
                investigator and will have the authority to punish
                Gomorrah's enemies as I see fit.

OLD WOMAN: You must be tired. Come, lay your head on my
                lap.

YOUNG GIRL: Her lap is as hard as a rock. Lay your head on my
                lap.

OLD WOMAN: I have a lap, too.

CITIZEN 1:   And I have a head too.

CITIZEN 3:   The way I cursed Sodom and spit on its gods, they
                ought to make me a great lord here.

CORRUPT: You can't tell the Leader what to do. From what
                you just said – you can tell you're still Sodomites
                at heart.

CITIZEN 3:   I see: you want the reward for yourself. I was
                already saying bad things about Sodom when you
                were still crawling around on all fours.

OAF: If I ever spoke against Gomorrah, it was only
                because they paid me. I never uttered a single bad
                word of my own free will.

CORRUPT: Tell them the whole truth. If you're useful, they'll forgive you.

OAF: In Sodom, I knew every street, every alleyway, every man, every woman. Here I'm in a foreign city and, what's more, I'm blind and hungry.

CORRUPT: We're all hungry.

CITIZEN 2: Why aren't they giving us any food?

CORRUPT: They haven't investigated you yet and don't know exactly who you are – so they don't give you any food. Why should they waste food on an enemy?

CITIZEN 3: But we're not their enemies.

CORRUPT: Friends must be able to go hungry for the good of the city and its Leader.

It's quiet. The men lean their heads on the women's laps.
BACKSTABBER sits and watches everything with a blank stare.
Suddenly, he coughs.

CITIZEN 1: Who's that? Is there someone else here?

CORRUPT: Who are you? Why are you so quiet? (No answer) Are you mute or what?

YOUNG GIRL: Can someone mute cough?

OLD WOMAN: I never thought about that.

YOUNG GIRL: Even sheep can cough.

CORRUPT: Why aren't you answering?

CITIZEN 2:   Maybe he's a spy?

CITIZEN 3:   I didn't say anything I shouldn't have.

CORRUPT: Can it be that we're blind and he's mute?

CITIZEN 3:   That was a cough from someone who has a voice.

CORRUPT: Let's hit him and see what he does. *(Starts to move blindly towards BACKSTABBER)* Where is he?

BACKSTABBER is chained to the wall. They approach him.

YOUNG GIRL: Here he is.

CORRUPT: Where? Grab him! There he is! Hey – answer when you're spoken to.

BACKSTABBER is silent and CORRUPT starts to hit him

OLD WOMAN: He's mute.

CORRUPT: We'll see soon enough. Hit him! Knock him out!

Everyone except for FIRST CITIZEN falls upon BACKSTABBER. They hit him, scratch him, poke him, slap him.

BACKSTABBER: What do you want from me?

VOICES: He's not mute!

CORRUPT: That voice is familiar . . . I know him!
                  (Suddenly) Backstabber!!

BACKSTABBER: Yes?

CORRUPT: You traitor, you dog. So the judges threw you
                  back across the border! How are you still alive?

VOICES: You know him?

CORRUPT: Do I know him? Of course I know him. I'm the
                  one who sent him to the judges in Sodom.

BACKSTABBER: You're here too – and blind to boot.

CORRUPT: I went blind as part of my work for Gomorrah –
                  and the Leader will know how to reward me. Your
                  time is almost up.

BACKSTABBER: How did all of you go blind at once? I don't
                  understand. . .

CORRUPT: A spy from Canaan threw some kind of poison on
                  us that made us blind.

YOUNG WOMAN: Two old spies with white beards.

BACKSTABBER: Your eyes are fine – and open.

CITIZEN 3:   Sodom's enemies want to make us all blind. That's
                  how they plan to bring about Sodom's destruction
                  and Gomorrah's victory.

CORRUPT: It won't work. (Pause) Well, Backstabber, did it
                 pay to betray Gomorrah?

BACKSTABBER: Get away from me, blind dog.

CORRUPT: You still have some teeth left, don't you. . .

BACKSTABBER: Get away, you leper!

CORRUPT: Everyone serves, and everyone betrays. Now
                 everyone's betrayed him.

BACKSTABBER: There's only one friend who never betrays you.

YOUNG WOMAN: Who's that?

BACKSTABBER: The one who's good and dead.

CORRUPT: This is just the beginning. When I come to power
                 tomorrow morning, you'll see that your friend
                 won't come so quickly. You'll wait a long, long
                 time for him to show his face.

BACKSTABBER: You rat! *(Spits on him)*

CORRUPT: That spit will cost you dearly. You're all
                 witnesses!

Everyone bangs on the door. The guard, SAVAGE, arrives.

SAVAGE: Well, how are your new lodgings? In Sodom,
                 penniless guests sleep in the street. Here, the state
                 gives them an apartment!

CITIZEN 1:   Just yesterday I heard someone say he slept in the
                  street in Gomorrah.

SAVAGE: Who?

CITIZEN1:   An old man, a spy from Canaan, the one who
                  made us blind.

SAVAGE: If we'd known he was here, he wouldn't have slept
                  in the street. First we would have put him up here
                  – and later given him a permanent place in the
                  cemetery, where all the spies live.

CITIZEN 2:   The spy made us blind. We crossed the border by
                  mistake. They've locked us up. Where's the
                  justice?

SAVAGE: Is there more justice in Sodom?

CITIZEN 2:   That's why I've always been on Gomorrah's side.

SAVAGE: While you were in Sodom, you spit on Gomorrah.
                  But suddenly you're our friends. Sure.

CORRUPT: Allow me, comrade, to speak. I'm Corrupt,
                  Gomorrah's messenger in Sodom, its foremost
                  informer. I was the one who informed on this dog
                  bound to the wall. We all turned blind while I
                  was speaking out against Lot and the spies from
                  Canaan. I'll tell you everything that happened and
                  give testimony about every person here.

SAVAGE: Since when am I your comrade? Did we fatten up
                  pigs together?

CORRUPT: I'm Corrupt – Corrupt!

SAVAGE: I'm not deaf. So what if you're Corrupt?

CORRUPT: There must be some mistake. You've never heard
               of me? Don't you know what I've done in Sodom?
               What's your rank? Send in a senior official.

SAVAGE: Who and what I am is none of your business. At
               the moment you're a prisoner – and I'm your
               master.

BACKSTABBER: Not a friendly welcome for Gomorrah's foremost
               informer.

CORRUPT: There's been a mistake.

SAVAGE: Mistakes are made in Sodom – not Gomorrah.
               Hey, you, tall guy, what's your name?

CITIZEN 1:   Noash.

SAVAGE: You've been here before, you worked for us and
               ran off to Sodom. Right?

CITIZEN 1:   Yes.

SAVAGE: And this other one –

CITIZEN 3:   I put myself on the line for Gomorrah. I hate
               Sodom so much that Corrupt had to stop me from
               single-handedly starting a rebellion. I'm also the
               one who threw the first stone at Lot's house.

CITIZEN 2:   I threw the first stone.

SAVAGE: Don't argue, the second stone is as good as the
                first. You'll throw many more stones here.

CITIZEN 3:   I don't understand.

SAVAGE: We need hard labor, and who else should do it but
                newcomers? Your life in Sodom made you impure.
                Your work in Gomorrah will cleanse you.

CITIZEN 2:   What kind of work?

SAVAGE: Breaking stones.

CITIZEN 2:   I'm too old for that.

SAVAGE: We don't work you to death, just to the end of
                your life

CITIZEN 3:   That's no work for me.

SAVAGE: You'll get used to it. It's hard at first. It's hot at
                the Dead Sea, no shade to hide from the sun. You
                work from sunup to sundown, sometimes later,
                you don't get much to eat. But at least you're
                building Gomorrah. At night, after work, you'll
                study Gomorrah's teachings.

OAF: I'm a Sodomite. I demand to be sent back. I'm
                friends with the highest rulers. I was Princess
                Nasty's dance teacher. I'm friends with the famous
                Bitchy who chopped off Looter's head. There's
                nothing for me here. I'm here by mistake.

SAVAGE: Gomorrah makes no mistakes.

OAF: Sodom will stand up for me.

SAVAGE: You're the one who's mistaken, young man, Sodom does not stand up for anyone. We've kidnapped many of its people. We've tortured them, killed them. But the Sodomite rulers haven't gone to war. Sodom forgets quickly – or makes itself forget.

OLD WOMAN: What will you do with us?

SAVAGE: You'll break stones.

OLD WOMAN: Women – break stones?

SAVAGE: In Gomorrah, women are equal to men – and have to do the same work.

WOMAN: We're not strong enough.

SAVAGE: You'll break smaller stones, and, just so you know, you're fed based on the number of stones you break.

CITIZEN 3: Is this how Gomorrah treats its friends?

SAVAGE: We need stones, not friendship. We need to build towers and erect walls.

CORRUPT: What's going to happen to me?

SAVAGE: You've asked a good question, and believe me, I
                  don't like having to answer you this way, but I
                  don't like to put things off. We know about
                  everything you've done, your riling up of crowds
                  in Sodom, all of your informing. You've earned
                  our reward, but you will receive none. On the
                  contrary, we have to do something that gives us
                  no pleasure.

CORRUPT: What?

SAVAGE: We have a rule which says that those who are no
                  longer useful are harmful.

CORRUPT: What are you saying? I gave my life for you. I
                  delivered scores of enemies into your hands.

SAVAGE: You're blind.

CORRUPT: I went blind for Gomorrah.

SAVAGE: Yes, but you're still blind. And you went blind in
                  an unusual way. Your eyes have no wounds. It
                  makes it look like the Canaanite spies can make
                  miracles – that's against our teachings. You'll go
                  around Gomorrah telling everyone how you went
                  blind, and your story will cause our people to fear
                  Canaan or even to start believing in Abraham's
                  god. That's no good

CORRUPT: I won't say anything.

SAVAGE: We've decided that the best thing would be if you
                  were no longer here.

CORRUPT: What do you mean, "no longer here"?

SAVAGE: You did your part – and now you die.

CORRUPT: What?

SAVAGE: That's the decision.

CORRUPT: I don't believe it.

BACKSTABBER: Believe it.

SAVAGE: Quiet. He'll die – but with his good name intact. We'll add his name to the golden scrolls. He may even get a medal after he's dead. Maybe someday we'll erect a monument in his name. You, on the other hand, will die a traitor.

CORRUPT: This can't be real, it just can't be real! I'm still young! I could have been a defense lawyer in Sodom, a judge, had everything in the world – but I renounced it all for Gomorrah. It's a lie – I've never supported Sodom. I stole, murdered, denounced my own relatives, sent fake letters, gave the Sodomites a bad name, all for one reason: to help you. I did it all willingly. And now Gomorrah is going to kill me!

BACKSTABBER: Why can't you accept your own fate?

SAVAGE: He may be a dog, but he's asking the right question.

CORRUPT: It's too much!

SAVAGE: It's not my decision. It was decided by the Leader, praised be his name forever and ever.

CORRUPT: The Leader?!

SAVAGE: Yes.

CORRUPT: Then he's making a mistake.

SAVAGE: If you can speak that way about our Leader, you'll die like a dog, an enemy of our people, a spy from Sodom.

CORRUPT: I don't need your medals and monuments. Bastards!

SAVAGE: Take this! *(Beats him)*

CORRUPT: You tricked me! Liar!

SAVAGE: Go – to the gallows! *(Drags him away)*

BACKSTABBER: It was all worth it – just to be here and witness this.

YOUNG GIRL: What's going to happen to us?

OLD WOMAN: Gods of Sodom – why are you silent?

CITIZEN 3:   If this is what life brings – it isn't worth living! *(Starts banging his head against the wall)*

CITIZEN 1:   Don't kill yourself yet. You still have to deliver your quota of stones.

OAF: Can it really be that they know all this in Sodom and do nothing? We need a war. Sodom will come rescue us!

BACKSTABBER: Gomorrah will start the war.

We hear ABRAHAM's voice: "Repent, children, repent!"

VOICES: Who's that? Who is that?

CITIZEN 1: Where did that come from?

CITIZEN 2: Have they brought another prisoner?

BACKSTABBER: No.

YOUNG GIRL: It's the voice of the spy who blinded us.

ABRAHAM: *(Just his voice)* I'm no spy and I didn't blind you. That was my friend, God's messenger, and he will heal you if you repent.

FIRST CITIZEN: Again with repentance!

BACKSTABBER: What do you mean, repent?

ABRAHAM: *(Just his voice)* Recognize that you've sinned. Regret your evil deeds.

BACKSTABBER: I've never regretted anything.

CITIZEN 2: Where's the voice coming from? From behind the wall? They're testing us.

ABRAHAM: *(Just his voice)* God is testing you, not Gomorrah.
                My friend, God's messenger, gave me the power to
                speak to you. You cast stones at us and God took
                your vision. He can make you alive or dead, blind
                or seeing. Believe in him – in his justice and
                mercy – and he will protect you, and save a lot of
                innocent children for your sake.

CITIZEN 1:   Whoever or whatever you are: I don't believe in
                God or his miracles. I've lived my whole life
                without seeing a single miracle. The strong have
                conquered and the weak have bled. There's only
                one power in the world: the power of might.

OAF: Might is right – in Sodom, in Gomorrah, in
                Canaan, everywhere.

ABRAHAM: *(Just his voice)* In Noah's time, the generation of
                the flood also had power – and so did Babel's
                generation of dispersion. Who is mightiest of all
                generations?

OAF: And who gets beaten in every generation?

ABRAHAM: *(Just his voice)* I don't know everything, and the
                little I know, I cannot reveal. But good is
                rewarded. Those who are beaten are consoled. It's
                as certain as the sun in the sky.

CITIZEN 1:   They're testing us. Gomorrah's trying to fool us.
                It's one of their tricks.

YOUNG GIRL: If you can perform miracles, show us one now.

ABRAHAM: *(Just his voice)* The miracle will come tomorrow
              morning.

YOUNG GIRL: We'll repent then.

ABRAHAM: *(Just his voice)* It'll be too late.

WOMAN: It's already too late. We're lost, lost, lost...

ABRAHAM: *(Just his voice)* You aren't lost yet. . .

Curtain.

Scene 2

The middle of the night. SNITCHY'S HOUSE.

SNITCHY: Where on earth is Oaf? He followed me all day
              praising me and playing his drum. He should
              have come tonight for his reward.

BITCHY: Where is he? He was supposed to come and teach
              me to dance.

SNITCHY: They say he's teaching Lot's daughter to dance.

BITCHY: He's teaching everyone. They all love him. He's
              such a good dancer.

SNITCHY: There's so much that needs to be done here. Taxes
              are high, money's worth less and less. Sodom has
              plenty of thieves, but the treasury steals the most,
              converting our earnings into shadows and dreams.
              I inherited from my husband, I inherited from my

lover, but everything's gone. You wouldn't believe
how much debt I'm in.

BITCHY: What happened to your fortune?

SNITCHY: It's here, but it's also not here. I have land, but
                 nobody wants to buy it. I used to have slaves, but
                 they died from hunger and disease. I have
                 promissory notes, but everyone who issued them
                 went bankrupt. Collecting those debts and paying
                 off witnesses and going to court and bribing the
                 judges – it would cost more than I would get.
                 Why do you think I killed Looter? He didn't do
                 me any harm.

BITCHY: So why did you kill him?

SNITCHY: Because he was poor and he was driving rich men
                 away with his jealousy. I can't indulge in a poor
                 lover.

BITCHY: Now you can have anyone you want.

SNITCHY: Sure, but I don't want anyone. Men disgust me.
                 When a man kisses me, it feels like he's biting
                 me. Tenderness bores me. My body can't bear
                 being touched. I can't even pretend anymore.

BITCHY: What are you going to do?

SNITCHY: It's your turn

BITCHY: I love Oaf.

SNITCHY: You can love him – but it won't bring us any money.

BITCHY: I want us to have a child.

SNITCHY: I wanted a child too, once, but not any more. Why have kids? If it's a boy, he'll die in war, or in a duel, or simply at the gallows. Being a man never ends well. If it's a girl, she'll have to do the same things I do.

BITCHY: Our parents had children.

SNITCHY: And what did it give them? When I was a girl, they worked like mules. Our father wanted me to be able to dance, play the harp, learn the languages of Gomorrah and Admah and Zeboim and even Canaanite. When I got older and ran off with my lovers, I was ashamed of my parents as though they were lepers. I was even ashamed to be at their funerals.

BITCHY: I often think about death.

SNITCHY: You're still young. The day is long.

BITCHY: Not about me dying. About making someone else dead.

SNITCHY: It's not as pleasant as you think, or as people make it seem. The moment when you actually murder someone might be exciting, but then there's this emptiness. Ever since I got rid of Looter, I just can't sleep.

BITCHY: Are you having regrets or something?

SNITCHY: I never have any regrets. But I have this fear that
                 I'll fall into the abyss.

BITCHY: Seriously?

The door opens and BOOR enters.

BOOR: Good evening, ladies. Or should I say good
                 morning?

SNITCHY: Who are you?

BOOR: You don't remember me? I'm the court bailiff.

SNITCHY: What do you want? I've been released.

BOOR: I saw a light in the house, looked through the
                 keyhole, and saw you here. Something strange is
                 happening.

SNITCHY: Another murder? *(Yawns)*

BOOR: Lot has some visitors from Canaan – some guy
                 named Abraham and his friend. They've been
                 prophesying about the destruction of Sodom.

SNITCHY: *(Yawns)* You call that strange? People have been
                 talking about the destruction of Sodom for ages.

BOOR: They're saying it's going to happen tomorrow
                 morning.

SNITCHY: They always say that.

BOOR: They can make miracles. They made Corrupt
            blind – and Oaf too.

BITCHY: Oaf?

BOOR: Corrupt was talking about the destruction of
            Sodom and the rise of Gomorrah. Oaf came with
            his drum and began praising your beauty. A few
            passersby stopped to listen. Lot's uncle Abraham
            wanted to say something, but they threw stones at
            him. His friend came out and he made everyone
            blind.

SNITCHY: That's ridiculous.

BITCHY: Were you there?

BOOR: No, but everyone's talking about it. Lot and his
            family are getting ready to leave as soon as the
            morning star appears.

SNITCHY: He's such a Hebrew.

BITCHY: What's a Hebrew?

SNITCHY: It's hard to say. They come from Ur and they live
            in Canaan. They're restless and they don't let
            anyone else rest either. They babble about some
            kind of God that sits in the heavens. One of them
            supposedly destroyed his father's idols.

BOOR:	That's Abraham. He's the one who's now in Sodom.
SNITCHY:	Why did they let him in? First Lot came, now Abraham, soon hundreds more will show up. These foreigners will eat us up like locusts.
BOOR:	That's why I can't sleep.
SNITCHY:	Me neither. During the day I'm tired, but at night I wake up. As soon as I begin to drift off, I dream about blood, death, severed limbs. Long graves being dug. Sad laments. I wake up drenched in sweat.
BITCHY:	Where's Oaf?
BOOR:	They say the blind crossed the border into Gomorrah.
SNITCHY:	You keep saying crazy things. Go, Boor, things are strange enough without you.
BOOR:	Please let me stay a little longer. I can't be alone.
SNITCHY:	You too?
BOOR:	I need to talk. I'm afraid of quiet.
SNITCHY:	Do you have a wife? A lover?
BOOR:	I have both, but I'm still alone. My wife is with her lover, and my lover went home to her husband.

SNITCHY: I'll bring you some wine. *(Leaves)*

BOOR: (To Bitchy) So you can't sleep either?

BITCHY: Tell me: do you know the Sodomite laws?

BOOR: Sodom has no laws.

BITCHY: Be serious. I'm not a child.

BOOR: I know the letter of the law better than the judges.

BITCHY: How long are people considered minors?

BOOR: Until the age of eighteen, but it can be lengthened. . .

BITCHY: What would happen if I killed you?

BOOR: I'd die.

BITCHY: Would I be put on trial?

BOOR: The books have no laws for pretty young women like you.

BITCHY: Please, be serious.

BOOR: They can't hang you, but they can fine you.

BITCHY: You call me pretty, but do you really like me?

BOOR: Everyone in Sodom is in awe of your beauty.

BITCHY: Would you help me kill someone?

BOOR: Why should I help you? I'm an officer of the law.

BITCHY: Do you need money?

BOOR: Who doesn't?

BITCHY: Can you keep a secret?

BOOR: Sure.

BITCHY: I want to kill my sister!

BOOR: Snitchy?!

BITCHY: I have no others.

BOOR: Why would you want to do that?

BITCHY: She controls everything. She takes all the money, all the glory, all the presents. Now she wants me to support her too. But it's not just that. . .

BOOR: So what is it?

BITCHY: Ever since everyone started saying that I chopped off Looter's head, I've wanted to actually kill someone.

BOOR: Do you have to kill your sister? Why not one of your servants?

BITCHY: What's the point of killing a servant? I want to
           kill her. I think about it all day and all night. I
           don't want her to take care of me anymore. I want
           to take her place: her bed, her clothing, her
           jewelry, her friends. When I imagine how her
           head will look lying on the ground, and all of
           Sodom coming to gape, I feel tingling down my
           spine.

BOOR: You don't talk like a minor.

BITCHY: I've grown up.

BOOR: Does she have an heir besides you?

BITCHY: I'm her only heir.

BOOR: Then you'll be able to bribe your way out.

BITCHY: Will you help me?

BOOR: What will I get?

BITCHY: Money. Why – what do you want?

BOOR: You.

BITCHY: I belong to Oaf.

BOOR: Oaf is blind – and in Gomorrah. He's dead twice
           over.

BITCHY: Is this your price?

BOOR: That's the price.

BITCHY: Then you can have me. What's your answer?

BOOR: When?

BITCHY: Tonight.

BOOR: What do I need to do?

BITCHY: Hold her head down. I'll chop it off.

BOOR: Do you have an ax?

BITCHY: I have her ax.

BOOR: Fine.

SNITCHY enters.

SNITCHY: Fortunes have changed. The servants are asleep
                   while the masters are awake. Here's your wine,
                   Boor. What were you two talking about?

BOOR: How old is your sister?

SNITCHY: Fourteen.

BOOR: A child with an adult's mind..

SNITCHY: What did she say?

The door opens as BASTARD and GUZZLER enter.

BASTARD: What are you doing here?

BOOR: I can't sleep, sir, so I took a walk. I saw the lights on.

SNITCHY: What are you doing here in the middle of the night?

BASTARD: Something's happened but I'd rather not speak with him here. Go, Boor.

BOOR: If you're talking about Lot, I already know.

GUZZLER: What do you know?

BOOR: About Abraham and his friend and how he struck Corrupt and Oaf blind.

BITCHY: So it's true?

GUZZLER: Go to sleep, Bitchy. Girls your age shouldn't be up all night.

SNITCHY: She's changed. She doesn't sleep at night, she drinks wine. All she talks about is murder.

GUZZLER: Be careful, Snitchy. She could prove you right.

SNITCHY: I'll be murdered one way or another. A fortune teller told me so.

BOOR: I'm going now. Goodbye, Snitchy. Goodbye, sir. *(Bows)*

BITCHY: Goodbye, Boor. *(She winks toward him, gives him a sign)*

SNITCHY: Go to sleep, Bitchy.

BITCHY: All right, I'm going, but I'm not going to sleep tonight. *(Leaves)*

SNITCHY: Why are you here?

GUZZLER: We might kick Lot out of court.

SNITCHY: What was Boor saying about people going blind?

GUZZLER: Something happened.

BASTARD: People are predicting the destruction of Sodom. Lot's making his family get out of town and leave everything behind. They're packing as if their house were on fire.

GUZZLER: His uncle has everyone panicking. He keeps talking about repentance.

SNITCHY: What's that?

BASTARD: I don't know – and I don't want to know.

GUZZLER: Someone has to finish off Lot. But it has to be done according to the law.

SNITCHY: You're the law.

BASTARD: Snitchy, we need your help.

SNITCHY: How can I help you?

BASTARD: Lot has a good reputation in Sodom. We can't
            knock him off on the street, so I want to round up
            all the other Hebrews and Canaanites living here.
            Come to court tomorrow and testify that he's a
            spy.

SNITCHY: Why me? Does Sodom have a shortage of liars?

BASTARD: You're important. If you say it, people will believe
            you.

GUZZLER: It's not what's said but who says it that matters.
            Say he met one a ruler from Gomorrah in your
            house.

SNITCHY: No one's going to believe that. Lot's not foolish
            enough to do that.

BASTARD: No one has to believe you. People like lies, but
            they have to come from the right mouth.

SNITCHY: What's in it for me?

BASTARD: We're going to seize his property, and kill all the
            other Canaanites while we're at it. They have a lot
            of money and Sodom could use a fresh start. We
            need a sacrifice. We're going to build a bonfire
            and burn them all.

GUZZLER: Gomorrah grew strong through fake trials too.
            Snitchy, you'll be renowned not only as a beautiful

woman experienced in love and murder, but also
as a protector of Sodom.

BASTARD: You'll be one step away from being a goddess.

SNITCHY: All this is making me lightheaded. But if this is
                what you want, I'll do it.

BITCHY: *(Enters)* I can't sleep, I can't sleep!

SNITCHY: What is it, little one, why are you so pale? What's
                that look in your eyes? *(Kisses her)*

BITCHY: I want to sleep – but I can't stop thinking!

SNITCHY: Thinking about what?

ABRAHAM: *(Just his voice)* Repent, people of Sodom, repent.

SNITCHY: What's that?

BITCHY: Who's saying that? What does that mean –
                repent?

ABRAHAM: *(Just his voice)* Turn away from your sins. Do not
                murder, do not steal, do not bear false witness.
                God, creator of heaven and earth, hates evil. I'm
                warning you for the last time: reject evil. If not,
                Sodom will sink.

GUZZLER: That's Abraham.

BASTARD: Where is he? Where's he shouting from? *(Looks
                through the window)*. I don't see anyone.

SNITCHY: Strange things are happening.

BASTARD: That Hebrew – he's hiding somewhere and shouting. He's trying to scare the whole city.

GUZZLER: We're not so easily unnerved.

BASTARD: Come to court tomorrow and bear witness against Lot. We'll clean up this whole mess.

ABRAHAM: *(Just his voice)* There won't be any tomorrow for you.

BASTARD: We're leaving. Good night, Snitchy, good night, Bitchy. *(They both leave)*

BOOR: *(Entering)* Now, Bitchy?

BITCHY: Now or never!

SNITCHY: *(Frightened)* Why did you come back?

BITCHY: Grab her!

SNITCHY: What do you want? What do you want? Sister!

BITCHY: Quickly!

BOOR grabs SNITCHY by the hair and drags her into the other room.

SNITCHY: *(Yells)* Murderers! . . . Gods! Protect me!

BITCHY: *(Picks up a hidden ax)* I have to do this!

BITCHY runs into the other room. We hear a heart-rending cry.
CURTAIN.

Scene 3

A meadow behind Sodom. LOT, his daughters, his WIFE, the
MAID, ABRAHAM, and the FRIEND walking with donkeys
carrying packs.

LOT'S WIFE: I told you – your uncle is crazy. It's just a day like
                  any other. The sun's rising over Sodom – while
                  we've left everything behind like idiots. I'm going
                  back!

ABRAHAM: Don't go. Sodom will be destroyed.

FRIEND: It's too late for repentance. God has already
                  opened the gates of fire and brimstone. They will
                  soon descend upon Sodom and Gomorrah, Adma
                  and Zeboim.

LOT'S WIFE: There's no fire and no brimstone. Foolish prattle
                  from two old dreamers. Everyone in Sodom will
                  laugh at us. They're already laughing.

ELDEST: Mother, I forgot my red sandals with the silver
                  buckles.

YOUNGEST: I forgot my Egyptian bracelet!

LOT'S WIFE: This is crazy. Maid, go back and see what's
                  happening. Did you lock up the house?

MAID: Why bother having a key in Sodom?

LOT'S WIFE: Did you close the shutters?

MAID: The thieves aren't afraid of locks and shutters.
You know that, ma'am.

LOT'S WIFE: Go back, Maid, and wait for us. We'll be back
soon. We'll be humiliated, but maybe we can save
some of our belongings.

MAID: I don't want to die.

LOT'S WIFE: You believe in this foolishness too?

MAID: Yes.

LOT'S WIFE: What happened to all of you? You've gone crazy.
Two drifters from Canaan show up – and everyone
goes insane.

LOT: I wouldn't have believed if I hadn't seen how he
(pointing to the FRIEND) struck them blind. A
person who can do such things ought to be
believed.

ELDEST: Mother, it's good to get out of the city. It's quiet,
the sky is clear. The birds are singing. Do you
hear them, mother?

LOT'S WIFE: I do hear them, I don't hear them. What's the
difference? I couldn't shut my eyes all night. I'm
tired. Never in my life have I had to wake up so
early. Maid, bring me a cushion.

MAID: Here.

LOT'S WIFE: Oh, I'm so tired. *(Yawns)* I can't stop thinking
               about Bastard and Guzzler. They're going to
               laugh when they hear what we've done. Everyone
               will be laughing their heads off.

LOT: Sodom's still asleep.

LOT'S WIFE: Sodom sleeps, but the thieves are awake! They'll
               clean us out. We'll come back to nothing. Maid,
               I'm thirsty.

MAID: Wine?

LOT'S WIFE: So early? No.

MAID: Water?

LOT'S WIFE: Not that either. I'd give away half my life to be
               lying in bed right now with you, Lot, or with
               anyone else. What's this? A snake?

LOT: A dead snake.

LOT'S WIFE: Look where you've dragged me, to snakes and
               thorn bushes. Why is everything so red?

LOT: Because of the sun.

LOT'S WIFE: Red like blood! The sun, like people, is born in
               blood and dies in blood.

LOT: In some countries people die in bed.

LOT'S WIFE: Women, not men. Every woman in Sodom is a widow. That's how it should be. Men should earn their wealth then turn it over to us.

YOUNGEST: Oh mother, the way you talk!

LOT: Your mother can hardly wait for me to die.

LOT'S WIFE: You've lived too long, Lot. You're a Hebrew and a coward. It's because of you that I'm lying on the hard ground right now. I was wanted by Sodom's best young men, but my father chose a Hebrew instead. *(Suddenly)* Lot, I'm going back.

LOT: Don't!

FRIEND: How many times do you need to be warned? God is infinite, but his patience has limits.

LOT'S WIFE: You're a fool and your god is a fool! It's a quiet morning like any other. I wish I were in bed, lost in sweet dreams. Maid, you would be bringing me milk with honey and fresh baked cookies. But instead, I'm lying in the dirt, unwashed, no makeup. Come, children, let's go. *(Gets up)*

ABRAHAM: Don't be so stubborn, please. Wait an hour.

LOT'S WIFE: I'm not waiting. Children, let's go.

ELDEST: Mother, let's wait an hour.

YOUNGEST: Let's wait.

LOT'S WIFE: Wait as long as you want. I'm going. Maid, come
                with me.

MAID: I told you, mistress, I'm afraid.

LOT'S WIFE: I order you to come with me!

MAID: I don't want to die.

LOT'S WIFE: And you, Lot, you're just going to stand there and
                listen to this backtalk? Kill her!

LOT: You just called me a coward.

LOT'S WIFE: What are you? Men? Or lambs? I'm warning you
                for the last time: Maid, come with me!

MAID: I'm afraid!

LOT'S WIFE: You won't have to be afraid much longer. *(Pulls
                out a dagger on her)*

MAID: Stop! Help! Help!
LOT: *(Grabbing the dagger from his WIFE)* Do
                whatever you want — but not this.

LOT'S WIFE: Fine. I'm going. But don't bother coming back to
                me. It'll be your death and burial.

ELDEST: Mother!

YOUNGEST: Mother!

LOT'S WIFE: I'm not your mother and you're not my daughters
               anymore. I'm starting a new life. I've never had a
               husband. My womb never gave birth to anyone.
               (Grabs a pack and leaves)

LOT: Where are you going? *(Holding his head)* Uncle,
               look what you've done to us.

ABRAHAM: It's not my fault.

LOT'S WIFE disappears. Long pause.

ELDEST: Father!

YOUNGEST: Father!

*LOT hugs his daughters and they stand together with their backs to
the audience*

MAID: What happens now? *(Hiding her face in her
               hands)*

*Thunder and lightning. Sodom is destroyed. It grows dark, and
when it's light again, they are all kneeling.*

LOT: My wife!

ELDEST: Our mother!

YOUNGEST: Mother!

FRIEND: You don't have a mother anymore. She's turned
               into a pillar of salt.

LOT: What am I supposed to do now? *(Weeps with his daughters)*

FRIEND: Well, Abraham, I delivered my message. I must go.

ABRAHAM: A harsh sentence. A terrible punishment.

FRIEND: Are you more compassionate than your Creator?

ABRAHAM: God's wisdom can be seen. But how can we understand his mercy? It would be better for me to be silent.

FRIEND: The time for speaking is long past.

ABRAHAM: And the time for prayer?

FRIEND: The time for prayer is never over. Everyone prays: the living, the dead. Corpses lie in their graves and pray.

ABRAHAM: Do you also pray?

FRIEND: We are made of prayer.
ABRAHAM: And God hears all of these prayers?

FRIEND: God prays too.

ABRAHAM: To whom?

FRIEND: To God.

ABRAHAM: How is that possible?

FRIEND: God is like an ever-growing spring that renews itself every day. The God of today prays for the God of tomorrow.

ABRAHAM: How can something eternal grow?

FRIEND: Eternity grows too.

ABRAHAM: I don't understand, but I'd better not ask. Whatever you have to say, say it plainly.

FRIEND: I cannot say any more. Your bond with God is about truth, not revelation.

ABRAHAM: Sometimes so much darkness falls over us that we can't go on without revelation.

FRIEND: Learn to live in darkness.

ABRAHAM: How long, Angel?

FRIEND: Until God no longer needs people's prayers.

ABRAHAM: God needs them?
FRIEND: Yes, Abraham. Now be well – peace be with you and your seed and all the strangers who may come to you and learn what you have to teach (leaves).

ABRAHAM: I've seen God! I've seen God! *(Kisses the ground)*

LOT: Where? Why doesn't God say anything to me?

ABRAHAM: You heard God's words. You saw God's hand.
             What else do you want?

LOT: What did God's hand give me? It burned my
             belongings, killed my wife. I'm a wanderer, a
             refugee. . .

ABRAHAM: God's refugee.

LOT: I don't know how to do anything – except for
             being a corrupt lawyer.

ABRAHAM: God's earth is plentiful. It will nourish you.

LOT: My hands were not meant for hard labor.

ABRAHAM: Be a shepherd and pasture your sheep.

LOT: That's not for me.

ABRAHAM: What is for you?

LOT: Cities, criminals, courts.

ABRAHAM: Go and find them.

LOT: Where are you going?

ABRAHAM: Back to Mamre.

LOT: You're abandoning me too!

ABRAHAM: It'll be better for you and better for me.

YOUNGEST: Yes. He should go.

LOT: Bless me, Abraham.

ABRAHAM: You've seen the truth. What else do you want?
               Walk in its light and God will bless you.

ELDEST: Who? The God of fire and brimstone? The God
               who killed my mother? A damning God cannot
               be a God who blesses.

ABRAHAM: The curses are blessings too. Goodbye.

LOT: Will we ever see each other again?

ABRAHAM: You and I will be reborn in each generation.
               (Leaves)

LOT: It's all lost. There's nothing left. There's a God in
               the heavens – but what does he want from me?

ELDEST: What's going to happen?

LOT: Eventually something will happen. *(Suddenly)*
               Sodom, I miss you!

ELDEST: Me too! *(Cries)*

YOUNGEST: Maybe it's not all gone. . .

LOT: We have a full wineskin. Maid, hand it to me.

MAID: Wine? Now?

ELDEST: Yes. Hand it over.

MAID: Here.

LOT: I need a drink. Otherwise I'll die. (drinks, falls
                 over drunk, sleeps).

YOUNGEST: Let's drink, Eldest.

ELDEST: And then what? We need a goal.

YOUNGEST: What kind of goal?

ELDEST: There are no men left for us.

YOUNGEST: There must be men somewhere.

ELDEST: We'll still need a man while we're looking. . .

YOUNGEST: True. But where can we find one?

ELDEST: Our father's a man.

YOUNGEST: You must be joking. . .

ELDEST: This is no time for jokes.

YOUNGEST: This is exactly what led Abraham's god to destroy
                 Sodom.

ELDEST: Sodom is gone. But whether Abraham's god did
                 it, or another god, I can't say for sure.

YOUNGEST: But Abraham and his friend foretold everything.

ELDEST: Maybe they were fortune tellers, or maybe they were given some sort of sign. I can't believe that Sodom was destroyed because it sinned.

YOUNGEST: Then why?

ELDEST: The Earth God is whimsical. He lets crops grow – then he burns them down. He gives birth to people and beasts – then he kills them. He's a blind god who doesn't know what he's doing. He's full of fire and smoke and terrible smells. That's what Corrupt taught me.

YOUNGEST: How did he know?

ELDEST: The Earth God is powerful but he has no mind of his own – he's a fool. Humans are smarter and we have to restrain him. That's what Corrupt said.

YOUNGEST: How can a person be smarter than a god?

ELDEST: Humankind is smarter – and is itself a god. It's the god of gods.

YOUNGEST: And look: the god of gods lies here drunk.
ELDEST: He's drunk, but he's a human being, and a man. We have no mother. He'll lie in our laps and we will bear his children. They'll grow and build a city.

YOUNGEST: What will they call it?

ELDEST: There's no better name than Sodom. . .

Darkness, then light. LOT sits with his daughters drinking. MAID serves them.

LOT: If Noah could drink, why can't I?

MAID:	Noah planted vineyards. But our wine will soon go sour.
LOT:	Noah had sons. I'm surrounded by women. Pass the cup, Maid. Everything on earth is cursed. But the fruit of the vine is blessed.
MAID:	As long as there's some left, I'll pour it (pours).
LOT:	We can't count on tomorrow. Especially since we have no tomorrow. Everything is behind us now. We can only look to the past.
MAID:	We have land. I took seeds with me. We can start over.
LOT:	Who is this "we"? Neither I nor my daughters are built to work.
MAID:	If no one wants to help me, I'll do it myself.
LOT:	The earth after the flood was moist. Here the earth is barren. The wind will cover everything with dust.
MAID:	Perhaps something can grow from dust.

ELDEST: Let tomorrow bring what it will. Today is ours.
            Isn't that so, Lot?

LOT: Yes.

ELDEST: You look so handsome, Lot. Your cheeks are red.
            Your eyes are glimmering.

LOT: Look how she talks to me! I'm your father, not
            your husband!

ELDEST: Is a father not a man?

LOT: I don't understand you. . .

YOUNGEST: Father, the world is gone. The earth has returned
            to the time of creation. We're back to the days of
            Cain and Abel.

ELDEST: Who did they copulate with? Who did Seth sleep
            with? Adam had no daughters. . .

LOT: It never occurred to me to ask . . . who?

YOUNGEST: Maybe their own mother?

LOT: What?
ELDEST: People back then had no inhibitions. They did
            whatever nature told them.

LOT: What do we know about what happened? Maybe
            Adam did have daughters?

YOUNGEST: If so, then brother lay with sister. . .

LOT: So it seems.

ELDEST: Why don't people do this today?

LOT: The old god was a good god. Abraham's god is
                spiteful. You saw what he did to Sodom and
                Gomorrah.

ELDEST: I saw Sodom burn, but I didn't see the hand that
                set it on fire.

LOT: Some hand did set it on fire.

ELDEST: Maybe it was a hand, maybe it was a foot, and
                maybe the fire lit up all on its own.

LOT: On its own?

YOUNGEST: In the desert, fires start all on their own. I've seen
                it.

ELDEST: She's right. Things happen on their own. Winds
                blow on their own. Hearts beat on their own.
                Trees grow on their own. Children die on their
                own. Maybe "on their own" is god.

LOT: How do you worship a god like that?

ELDEST: It doesn't need to be worshiped. You only need to
                worship yourself.

YOUNGEST: Did Corrupt teach you this?

ELDEST: He taught me a little – and the rest I figured out myself.

LOT: My dear daughters, you're smarter than your father. Or maybe the wine's confused me?

ELDEST: Put your head on my lap.

LOT: You're drunk.

ELDEST: You're not sober either. . .

YOUNGEST: Drink, father, drink. Our laps are just as soft as Snitchy's. Our lips are just as moist. Our loins. . .

LOT: Quiet!

ELDEST: We have no one but you, and you have no one but us. . .

LOT: What?

ELDEST: We have to create a new world.

LOT: Should a world be made this way?

YOUNGEST: How else can it be made? With your Aunt Sarah, who will soon be ninety?

LOT: And I thought Sodom had been destroyed. . .

ELDEST: Kiss me, Lot, kiss me.

LOT: You, daughter, are a true Sodomite!

YOUNGEST: Me too!

LOT: Sodom is dead. Sodom lives on. Now I see.

ELDEST: What do you see?

LOT: I see the sky, but I'm sinking into the abyss. I've
                 seen God, but I can't worship him. Death hangs
                 over my head but I lust for my daughters' breasts.

YOUNGEST: You'll live, father, you'll live.

ELDEST: We'll bring forth new generations from you.

LOT: You'll only cause me sorrow. . .

YOUNGEST: Drink a little more.

LOT: I'll drink to the last drop. Like this! (falls down)

ELDEST: It's now or never.

YOUNGEST: Who first, me or you?

ELDEST: I'll break any rule – but I won't give up my
                 birthright.

YOUNGEST: Sodom's most important rule.

*The lights go down and when they come up again LOT is asleep.
His daughters sleep on either side of him. MAID is nearby. LOT
opens his eyes.*

MAID: Sir, can this be?

LOT: Yes.

MAID: After everything you've seen and heard?

LOT: This is how it has to be.

MAID: What's going to happen to me?

LOT: I need children – and I need slaves too. I'll
               impregnate you and you'll give birth to slaves.

MAID: From your seed?

LOT: There's no other.

MAID: Why don't you pray to God? You heard what the
               man said. You saw his miracles.

LOT: I heard and I didn't hear. I saw and I didn't see. I
               believe and I don't believe.

MAID: I saw – and I heard – and I believe.

LOT: Keep your faith.

MAID: May I pray?

LOT: What do I care? *(Falls over and sleeps)*

MAID kneels, bends over, prays. CURTAIN.